Tackle Sailing

Tackle Sailing
Christopher Dawson

Stanley Paul, London

Stanley Paul & Co Ltd
3 Fitzroy Square, London W1

An imprint of the Hutchinson Publishing Group

London Melbourne Sydney Auckland
Wellington Johannesburg and agencies
throughout the world

First published 1959
Second impression 1961
Second revised edition 1968
Fourth impression 1972
Third edition 1977

Set in Monotype Times

Printed in Great Britain by The Anchor Press Ltd
and bound by Wm Brendon & Son Ltd
both of Tiptree, Essex

ISBN 0 09 128640 9 (cased)
     0 09 128641 7 (paper)

Contents

CONTENTS

Foreword

It has been my aim in writing this book to explain simply and
clearly how and why a boat sails, and what steps to take if
you want to own and sail your own boat. I have tried to
emphasize those things which help to build up a sense of the
sea, and not only deal with the sailing of dinghies. There are
other books which go into dinghy sailing in more detail, and
also on more advanced subjects such as cruising, navigation,
ship's husbandry and maintenance, and yacht design and
construction. I have given at the end of this book a list of
other books which I think will help the reader to carry on
where I have left off. In *Tackle Sailing*, however, I have tried
to include enough to start you sailing, and until you have
some practical experience under sail you are not likely to
learn a great deal more from books.

One of the snags which people new to sailing find difficult
to overcome is the peculiar language of those who have to do
with boats. Not only is it quite unlike anything spoken anywhere else, but it varies enormously from place to place and
from one person to another. In writing this book I have
defined a number of terms as I go along, and others will be
made clear by the diagrams, but I have brought together in
a glossary at the end all the purely nautical terms I have used
and included some others which you may come across elsewhere. I have tried to use and define the terms in the senses
which are common among sailing people, and I have
included some of the commonly found alternatives.

Apart from the explanation of the fundamental theory of sailing, most sailing instruction boils down to pointing out what may go wrong if you do things in the wrong way, and so you gain the impression that sailing is a risky business, fraught with discomfort, and that yacht harbours are constantly in a state of chaos. In fact, sailing is not in the least dangerous compared with many other sports, and you can be as adventurous or as cautious as you please and still have an immense amount of enjoyment. Damage to boats and gear may be expensive, but is relatively uncommon, and damage to crew more serious than a wetting is quite rare. Anyone being rescued from a yacht or dinghy, or the very occasional fatality, is news, and a report is invariably published in the Press, but considering how many people are on the water at weekends in the summer such incidents are quite exceptional. So don't let the warnings in this book discourage you from sailing, just bear them in mind when you do set out.

Foreword to the Third Edition

It has been a sobering experience for me to return to something I wrote nearly twenty years ago, years in which I have added to my sailing experience and learnt many lessons; years also in which the technological, social, commercial, and now we even have to add political, background to sailing has changed almost beyond recognition.

When I wrote the first edition wood was the normal material for boats, boats were built rather than manufactured, sailing people were relatively few and sailing waters much less congested. Sailing schools as we now know them did not exist. What is now the Royal Yachting Association, with excellent training and qualification schemes for people who want to sail dinghies or cruisers, was still a body concerned only with racing. There were far fewer attempts by authority to tell us what we ought and ought not to do for our own safety and that of others, and the idea of a punitive tax levied on boats and their equipment, at a special rate indicating that they are luxury goods, had not occurred to the sternest of Chancellors of the Exchequer.

But despite all these changes to the incidentals the fundamentals of sailing and the sea remain much the same, and I am relieved to find that much of what I wrote as a younger man is still relevant. Nevertheless, revising the book for this edition has meant re-writing about half of it completely, and providing many new illustrations. In doing this revision, in a time when specialization has attacked sailing as much as any field of activity, I have increased the concentration on one particular approach to the subject – the approach which is likely to suit those who want to sail for the pleasure of being at sea (or afloat elsewhere) and of exercising the skills of seamanship. So I have tended to write about boats which lend themselves to pottering rather than dashing round the buoys, to cruising rather than to the costly extravagance of 'ton-cupping'. I believe that this is the kind of sailing which attracts the greater number of people, but which tends to be less publicized than the competitive sort so may be missed by the newcomer. And as in the first edition I have had very much in mind the needs of people without much money to spend.

1. Types of Boats and Where to Sail Them

Sailing is a pastime which is quite different from any other: it means so many different things to different people. For some it is just a Saturday afternoon sport, and for others it is a complete way of life which involves making a permanent home out of a boat. But there are two basically different approaches to sailing, that of the racing man and that of the cruising man. The first likes to pit his boat and skill against that of others, straining to get the best possible performance out of his boat, and rarely putting out except to race. The second likes to solve the problems of getting from one place to another, and enjoys the ever-changing conditions of wind and water for their own sake, and as a challenge to his skill. Both must know the fundamentals of sailing, and many a cruising man has learnt much from the occasional race.

This book is written for the beginner without much money, and for him the best boat to start with is a small one, a dinghy or other open boat in fact, because it is cheap to buy and run, and presents all the fundamental problems of sailing without the confusion of elaborate and heavy sails and rigging, and the necessity for careful navigation, which go with a larger craft.

Sailing Dinghy Types

Sailing dinghies range from shapeless and heavy boats, which can barely be persuaded to sail, to light and delicate racing craft which can attain near-speedboat speeds but which have to be handled like racehorses. Prices, new and second-hand, range accordingly (in 1976) from under £100 to over £1000. One of the slow and heavy sort will soon tire the patience of the ordinary mortal, and is not really much safer, as its poor performance makes it difficult to get it out of awkward corners. The more thoroughbred types of racing dinghy are likely to be too expensive and too tricky to handle. There are many types which fall between these two extremes.

Dinghies intended mainly for racing fall into two categories: one-designs and restricted classes. They differ in the latitude for change of shape, rig and equipment allowed to the designer, builder and owner. One-design boats are kept as nearly identical as practicable, while restricted classes are governed by limiting dimensions and other rules, but allow more scope than one-designs for improvement.

There are some dinghy classes which, although used for racing, are simple and sturdy and well suited to the beginner whatever kind of sailing he wants to do. Examples are the minute Optimist (best suited to small children on their own), the ubiquitous Mirror (suitable for two teenagers), the still popular GP14, and the Bosun.

Although there is still a scarcity of really good open-boat designs aimed at the potterer, some companies have specialized in this field. Among the most attractive boats of this kind are the Drascombe range from Honnor Marine of Totnes, which go from 15 to 22 feet (4·6 to 6·7 metres) in length. It has to be admitted, however, that these boats – though open – are far from cheap.

There is a process of natural selection at work among boat designs, and although there is a constant stream of new ones, only a few prove really successful. It is wise for the beginner to seek out one of these, and not to be too ready to fall for the attractions of the latest model seen at a boat show. In in a way not found in more open waters. Long distances are usually broken up by locks, which are a nuisance, and some sections of the Thames, in particular, become so congested in the summer that sailing can become rather frustrating. Finally there are reservoirs and disused chalk and gravel pits. Some of these are nowadays being made available to sailing clubs and can provide good racing: although most of them are limited in size they are usually a good deal wider than our rivers. If you want to explore rather than just race they would prove rather restricting. Much the same applies to most British natural lakes outside the Lake District and Scotland.

In most cases it is best to keep a dinghy ashore. In nontidal waters she can be kept alongside a landing stage, but under some conditions she will probably bump about and damage herself, however well provided with fenders. A heavy boat will have to be kept afloat, and a boat which has to be kept afloat needs to be fairly heavy and stable, without too tall a mast, which might catch the wind and blow her over. Finding a good place to keep a boat ashore is not easy; it needs to be near the water, but preferably out of reach of the waterside small boy or vandal. It is best to rely on the facilities provided by the nearest club, and follow what the other members do. Most clubs catering for dinghies (and few don't these days) have either storage under cover or an open park behind a locked fence.

If you are going to sail from an open beach the boat must be light enough to be easily manhandled. A good area of deck and plenty of buoyancy are essential for safety, and the boat needs to be stable enough for the crew to be able to clamber in over the transom. Sail area should not be too small as control will have to be gained rapidly when launching from a lee shore, and it will in any case not be possible to set out in a strong onshore wind.

There are enormous local variations in conditions and in the ways of handling boats on beaches, and indeed in styles of mooring and accommodation ashore in all kinds of harbours. An old friend of mine successfully launches his Drascombe Dabber, which weighs about a quarter of a ton, from a steep shingle beach near his home, and hauls it up again in the way local fishermen have for generations if not centuries, except that he has coupled an electric motor to the winch he shares with two or three neighbours. A nearby headland gives some limited shelter from the prevailing westerly winds, and northerlies are offshore, but the beach is fully exposed to the south and east. This is typical of the situation on many parts of our coastline, and if such an area is conveniently situated it may well be the best one for you, to save a long journey, perhaps towing the boat on a trailer. But if there are no boats already using the beach regularly the chances are that there is a good reason for this and it would be unwise to make it your base. Boats for beach launching need to have battens or rubbers on the bottom to take the wear and tear on sand or shingle and the heavier the boat is the more necessary this will be.

Improvements in trailers and near-universal car ownership have opened up the possibilities of keeping a boat at home, even if she is big enough to have a cabin, and trailing her to whatever sailing waters take your fancy. But it is not always easy to find a good place to launch a boat from a trailer, so it is as well to make local inquiries first. The local harbourmaster or coastguard will usually be most helpful in matters of this kind, and their advice about whether conditions of wind and tide are suitable for launching from a particular site should be sought and respected. Alternatively local yacht and sailing clubs can be consulted, but many have no permanent staff so it is not always easy to contact them. Most small boats can be trailed, and some larger ones too, but handling is easier if they are fairly flat-bottomed. Trailers themselves need to be properly engineered and have to conform with various road regulations relating to dimensions, weight, braking and lights. It is possible to carry a really small boat on the rack on the roof of a car, but watch the car manufacturer's recommended maximum roof-load.

I have considered open beaches first because they are so widely found around our coasts. But there are many small harbours which provide sheltered launching sites, and even the possibility of keeping a boat afloat or in a berth where she will dry out at low tide. But space is often limited, and charges may be considerable. In any case exploration and discussion with the local harbourmaster is essential before you commit yourself to the regular use of such a harbour.

Larger commercial ports are usually dirty, and most discourage small private craft. Some, however, do have corners where they can be accommodated. Again a visit of inspection and the taking of local advice is called for.

Perhaps the best place for a small boat is a creek or estuary too shallow to attract larger boats, and this can of course provide both a place to keep your boat and a place to sail her. Usually there will be open sea within reach to tempt you out when you are feeling adventurous and conditions are right. Estuaries and creeks are suitable for almost any sort of boat and the choice will depend more on what exactly you want to do with the boat, and of course what local classes there are if you want to race.

On rivers and reservoirs problems of performance in a chop scarcely arise, though a large reservoir may have quite a popple on it in a really strong wind. The main things here are an easily driven hull, and plenty of sail area to make the most of the light and variable winds so often found inland.

Uses of Yacht Clubs and Schools

Clubs have many useful functions and it is well worth while for the beginner in sail to join one. Apart from somewhere to keep the boat they usually have changing-rooms, stores for gear, and a club-room which is often also a bar. Current copies of the yachting magazines are usually kept there. Moorings afloat are in many anchorages organized by the club. Although some clubs are called cruising clubs nearly all in fact organize races of some kind, and if you do want to race membership of a club is essential.

In clubs where most of the members are mainly interested in cruising, the committee usually feels impelled to lay on some sort of organized group activity, such as a 'cruise in company', but the cruising man is an incurable individualist and usually prefers to make his social contacts only in the bar. Subscriptions of small local clubs are usually quite modest and a letter to the Honorary Secretary from anyone keen to sail will probably bring an immediate welcome. Even if you have no boat of your own you can join a club and crew for other members. This is a good way to learn for a while, but does not always give you a chance to pick up the fundamentals.

It is as well to talk to one or two members before joining since a club can be a very personal thing, and if the members are not people you feel at home with belonging to that particular one would probably be a mistake. Clubs vary enormously in how helpful they are to beginners, and in the extent to which they offer instruction. Nowadays a good way to start sailing is to take one or more courses at a sailing school. These advertise in the magazines – it is wise to choose an RYA-recognized school.

Finding Your Boat

Having decided what sort of boat you need you must now set about finding her. For dinghies advertisements in the local paper, or pinned up in the club, are a likely lead for a second-hand boat. The yachting magazines also have advertisements, but as they cover the whole country there may be nothing in your district, and it is hardly worth going halfway across the country for a small boat.

For a new boat you may go to a local boatyard if they specialize in dinghies, but if they build mainly larger craft it is advisable to avoid them. If it is a class boat there may be a limited number of builders approved by the class association. In any case, advice can be had from other members of the local club.

There are four ways of acquiring a new boat: to have one built to order, to buy one that is ready built, either from a yard or manufacturer, or from a shop, to buy a kit from a firm specializing in boat kits, such as the Bell Woodworking Co. Ltd, or to build the boat entirely yourself. Unless you are an experienced woodworker the last is likely to be too much of an undertaking, but kit-built boats are very satisfactory, and cost about half as much as a complete boat, or even less. Under present regulations, however, VAT at a higher rate is charged on kits but only at standard rate on the uncut materials you buy to build your own boat.

If you have a room, garage or shed to work in in the winter the boat could be built during the bad weather and be ready to sail in the spring. In any case allow plenty of time so as to make a good job of it and still be ready for a full season's sailing. It is as well to remember that just because all the materials came in through the door it does not follow that the completed boat will come out. Many a window frame has had to be taken out, and even walls knocked down, to

21

extract a boat built without a few measurements being taken first.

If you decide to buy a new boat complete, and do not know of a suitable supplier in the vicinity, it will be worth looking further afield. Apart from the advertisement pages of the yachting journals one of the best places to find this sort of information is the London Boat Show, now held annually at Earls Court, early in the new year. There many of the builders, especially those specializing in small craft, have stands showing their work, and you can see the type of boat you are interested in. There is also a growing number of regional boat shows, one of the biggest being held annually in Southampton, in September. The local show may be nearer you, but you will probably find a much smaller choice of boats there than at Earls Court.

When buying a new boat it is as well to make sure what equipment is included in the price. Sails are often an extra, and may well add a substantial sum to the price.

Likely Troubles in Old Boats

Buying a second-hand boat presents the same traps for the unwary as buying anything else second-hand, and it is not difficult to make a boat which is in poor shape look superficially sound by careful paintwork.

Most small craft are moulded in glass-reinforced plastics (commonly called fibreglass), or are of glued plywood construction. Traditional construction was of separate planks fastened to a framework, but this is rarely seen in new boats now. However an older wooden boat may well be a good buy if it is in good condition, and many people find traditional construction much more aesthetically appealing than the modern methods.

Most defects in plastics boats are fairly obvious, taking

the form of physical damage ranging from fractures and holes to scores and chips, or surface cracks in the gel coat. Most can be fairly easily repaired if not too extensive. A generally shabby gel coat which has lost its shine can be made as good as new by carefully applied coats of polyurethane enamel over a properly prepared and primed surface. One thing to watch for is where double-skin construction is used with an inaccessible space between the skins. Unless this space is completely filled with plastics foam it is very likely that water will have got in, in which case it is very difficult to get out again. Rocking the boat from side to side or end to end may enable you to hear water splashing about in a trapped space. If this cannot be drained out it is a fault of design and I would be inclined to look elsewhere.

Proper marine plywood is durable, the most likely troubles being abrasion of the outer plies, cracking of panels due to impact, and failure of glued joints with other members. Exposed edges of plywood, showing end grain, are bad workmanship and lead to water absorption which can cause trouble. Delamination of ply can happen to good quality material as a result of this, but is more likely to be due to the use of a non-marine grade, which would be a good reason for not buying the boat.

Parts of a plywood boat will be in solid timber, and here much the same points apply as for a traditionally planked boat. Rot, the greatest enemy of larger wooden craft, is not so prevalent in open boats because they are better ventilated. Troubles to look for are cracks, showing that time and excessive drying out have made their mark, and bent frames with angles or fractures in them are common in clinker-built boats. The inside of the centreboard case is the most neglected spot as a rule and it is worth looking there for worm holes, soft timber, or excessive chafing. The bottom planking may be rubbed and scored through careless dragging up the beach. Sighting along the keel will show whether it is straight, or has a smooth curve. If not, the whole hull has distorted, and if it is a class boat it may no longer be within the required measurements. Knees, which stiffen the hull, often split or crack, and may be loose on their fastenings.

Provided large areas of the timber are not in poor condition it may be worth taking an old wooden boat despite some defects, especially if you are enough of a handyman to do the necessary repairs yourself. This applies particularly to a boat for pottering up and down the creeks, where class rules have not got to be met, and an old and substantially built boat may have the stability and room to move about that can make a day afloat a real pleasure.

The sails are the most important, and the most expensive, part of a boat's equipment. They deteriorate from two main causes: chafe and decay. Chafe will be obvious if the sail is passed through the hands and examined carefully. It is most likely to be found along the boltropes and cringles, and where the sail rubs on shrouds. Mildew attacks sails of natural fibre if they are left in warm damp conditions, and leaves its characteristic blackish pockmarks, but this material is now rarely used and sails are mostly of Terylene which is not damaged by mildew. Sometimes the Terylene gets brittle from old age or exposure to sunlight. This can be detected by piercing the sail with a sailmaker's needle, which has a thicker triangular part towards the point. If the sail is sound the fibres will be parted, but if brittle they will break, showing rough ends when the needle is withdrawn.

The condition of rigging is less important as it would be as well to renew it on taking over a second-hand boat, unless it is in very good condition. A dinghy's rigging can all be replaced for a modest sum.

Spars are usually of tubular aluminium alloy or light

wood such as Sitka spruce, British Columbian pine (Douglas fir) or other clean-grained softwood. Aluminium spars should preferably be anodized, because this gives them a hard, smooth finish which lasts for many years. Without this finish aluminium alloys are liable to corrosion which appears as whitish spots of abrasive deposit. This can be cleaned off and the spars painted with polyurethane for a durable finish. As with glass-reinforced plastics proper priming and preparation is essential for a good job.

Deep dents in the tube wall seriously weaken the spar, and may indicate that it has been bent and straightened without proper repair, in which case it is very likely to fail again. Other points to watch for are severe local corrosion around fittings attached to the spar – this may mean the fitting is of the wrong material, or fastened with the wrong kind of screw or rivet. In this case corrosion can proceed quickly and ruin the spar. If there is any way of seeing inside the tube it is well to check that there is no serious corrosion there either.

Wood spars soon show neglect, especially if varnished. Apart from worn patches, there may be discoloured areas where the weather has affected the wood. This may or may not indicate rot – if it does the wood will feel soft and spongy under pressure from a thumbnail. Longitudinal cracks in solid spars are relatively harmless, if undesirable, but transverse ones mean damage and weakness. Glued spars, whether solid or hollow, should not show signs of opening along the glue lines.

Can You Afford a Boat?

Yachts are thought of as luxuries, but small boats do not cost a great deal to buy or run. A small dinghy can be bought new for the cost of a colour television set, and with owner maintenance and careful treatment need not cost much more than the licence fee and repairs in upkeep, depending mainly on mooring costs. A larger open boat, such as a Drascombe Lugger, costs about as much as a small car to buy new and a good deal less to run.

With careful upkeep a boat holds its value better than many other possessions and a good boat will fetch a substantial proportion of its current cost new on the second-hand market. If you have the time and skill to renovate a shabby but basically sound boat, you can show quite a good profit and get some sailing between buying and selling. The same applies with home-built boats, provided they are to a reasonably professional standard of construction and finish.

2. Construction, Rig and Equipment

A variety of materials and methods of construction are used for sailing dinghies and other open boats, but the majority are now of glass-reinforced plastics or marine plywood. Hot or cold moulded plywood boats may be found on the second-hand market and there are still some traditionally built boats available both new and second-hand. Other plastics, including ABS, have been used, but as yet few sailing boats are produced in them. In general grp and plywood construction will give the best combination of qualities and I will be concentrating mainly on them. Other materials tend to be heavier if the boat is to be adequately strong, are often more expensive, and need more maintenance effort.

Most boats produced in quantity are in grp, because this is a good basic material, and the moulding techniques used with it lend themselves to economic production of quantities which suit the market.

Plywood boats are mostly of chine construction, that is the hull's shell is made from flat pieces of plywood bent to a curve longitudinally and straight, or nearly straight, in the transverse direction. This means incorporating one or more angles or chines where the panels join, and at these chines there are normally solid timber stringers forming part of the boat's supporting structure. In small dinghies the 'stitch and glue' joint is sometimes used at the chine. Most ply designs have been developed to cater for home construction from scratch or from a kit, but chine-built plywood boats are also available commercially.

Figure 2 Small Boat Construction Methods
(A few typical examples – there are endless variations in detail)

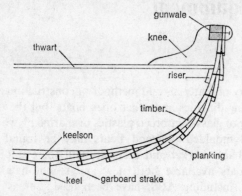

Traditional clinker. Carvel, which is not much used in dinghies, is similar but has planking edge-to-edge with caulking to seal the joint. This gives a smooth exterior and fewer dirt traps inside. Well built clinker is lighter and more robust.

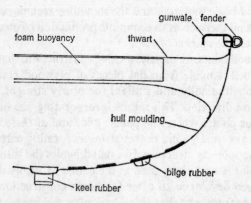

Simple grp with separate gunwale moulding and channel-section thwart bonded in.

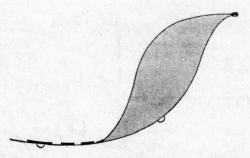

Double-skin grp with plastics foam buoyancy between shell mouldings.

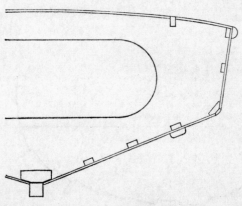

Marine ply chine construction with chine battens and web frames or bulkheads.

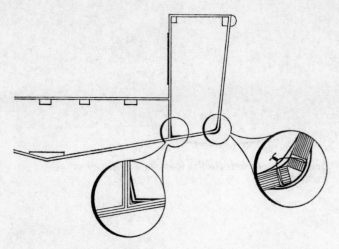

Light ply construction with lockers, built-in buoyancy and joints made with glass tape and resin. Chine is stitched with copper wire first.

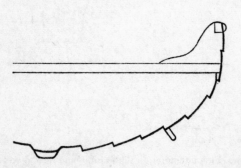

Grp simulated clinker with wood trim

The choice between the two main types is not easy: ply tends to be a little lighter but needs more maintenance. On balance I think grp makes a sensible choice for the beginner if he is buying a boat rather than building one. It is also possible to buy the bare mouldings of a grp boat and complete the job oneself, with quite a big saving on the final cost.

The constructional methods and arrangements of boats in modern materials are diverse and properly the province of the designer. The hull characteristics which will concern the beginner most will be stability and buoyancy when swamped.

Stability increases with beam (i.e. breadth) and particularly waterline beam. This means that a tubby boat will be less easily upset than a narrow one, but she will also tend to be slow. Sailing dinghies need to be broader than pure rowing boats to be able to stand up to the sideways forces imposed on them by the sails. For pottering a hull which has a flattish bottom and nearly vertical sides, blended with a nice round bilge, is best. Chine boats range from the completely flat bottomed (sometimes called flatties) to ones having one angle at the central keel and one or more angles or chines at the bilge (see Fig. 2).

The general characteristics of the hull are determined largely by the shape of the midship section, but there is scope for variation in the way the ends are drawn, and for most purposes reasonably full ends will suit the beginner, as they give more stability and carrying capacity.

Most dinghies are designed to be sailed upright, with their crew acting as mobile ballast to balance the heeling force of the sails. They can then be fine forward and flat aft, a combination which helps performance and planing. But once an asymmetrical form like this is heeled it presents an awkward shape to the water which slows down the boat and makes her difficult to steer. For this reason boats which are too large to be held upright by their crews sitting out are usually designed to have less extreme differences of form between bow and stern.

Buoyancy should be a permanent part of the boat in the form of air-tight boxes, preferably filled with plastics foam. Inflatable bags are widely used, and can provide plenty of buoyancy if properly fixed, but they are vulnerable and can come adrift. It is also easy to forget them if they are not kept permanently in the boat, and if they are they are liable to deterioration and damage. One can hardly have too much buoyancy, although the point can be reached where foot-room is short! Some of the volume can be in the form of lockers with air-tight lids (ideal for anything from sand-wiches to spare clothes – not forgetting flares and other necessary equipment) but enough permanently sealed buoyancy should remain so that the boat will still float with a good margin if she begins to capsize when the lids are open.

A Grip on the Water

All sailing boats need some sort of fin to give them a grip on the water, for reasons which I will make clear in Chapter 3, and by far the commonest way of achieving this in a dinghy is with a centreboard. This is a flat plate of metal, or a solid timber or plywood fin, so fitted that it can be raised into a box mounted on top of the keelson, and lowered when needed. Metal ones are also called centreplates. There is one kind which is slid bodily upwards and removed from the box, or centreboard case. This is called a daggerboard, the normal centreboard being pivoted about a bolt at the for-ward end of the centreboard case.

It is very important for the strength of the boat that the keel be amply wide to accommodate the slot, and that the case should be well braced by attachment to at least one

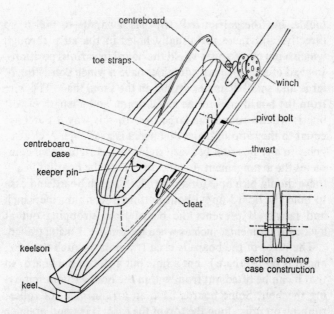

Figure 3 Typical centreboard arrangement

thwart. Sometimes a wooden boat that has been built only for rowing is converted into a sailing dinghy by the addition of a centreboard case, and if the slot is cut in the keel it is likely that not enough timber remains. This can be made good by gluing long strips on either side of the keel. An alternative is to have the centreboard slightly offset so that the slot comes in the planking beside the keel and not in the keel itself.

A centreboard is raised and lowered either by being formed into a lever at its upper forward end, with a tackle attached to it, or by wire span or strip of galvanized steel or other metal attached to the aft end. The wire span also goes to a tackle, but the galvanized strip has a handle to pull it up directly, and there are usually holes in the strip through which a pin can be put to hold the board in various positions. Instead of a tackle many dinghies have a winch consisting of large and small diameter drums on the same shaft. The wire from the board goes to the small drum, and a length of soft line is wound round the large one. In this way a purchase equal to the ratio of drum diameters is available. A cleat to belay in any position between right up and right down completes the arrangement. In all cases where the board is heavy there should be a hole for a pin right through board and case to hold the board up without putting a strain on the winch and tackle. It prevents the board from dropping out at awkward moments, such as when the dinghy is being trailed.

The pivot of the board is usually a bolt through the case, and it is best if there is not a hole but a slot in the board, so that it can be lifted out from within the boat without removing the bolt. Some boards have an arrangement of rollers running on rails along the top of the case. It is good practice to have the bottom of the slot in the keel covered by two strips of rubber insertion, butted together, to keep mud out of the case, steady the board, and prevent water being forced up through the case when sailing fast or being towed.

There is another way to give a dinghy a grip on the water which is very adequate for a boat which is only sailed occasionally, and that is a leeboard. This is a plank, usually slightly fan-shaped, which is hung over the lee side of the boat. Leeboards are common in some larger craft, particularly Dutch types and our own Thames barges, and here there is a board on each side, the lee one always being used when lateral resistance is needed. In a dinghy it is simpler and more satisfactory to have one symmetrical board which can be hung on either side. The gunwale must, of course, be adequately strong to take the wringing stresses set up by the board. These will be less if the board is supported by a chock at about water level as well as by the gunwale.

Also very important to the sailing boat is the rudder. Apart from steering the boat the rudder contributes to the grip on the water of the boat as a whole. Dinghy rudders are normally hung on pins which engage with eyes, these being known as pintles and gudgeons respectively. The rudder can then be lifted up and stowed inboard. The tiller normally fits into a socket on the rudder head, and in most dinghies has an extension fitted to it so that the helmsman can sit right out and still steer the boat. Many dinghy rudder blades are pivoted in the stock, in the same way as a centreboard, so that they can be raised and lowered. When raised the boat can be controlled in very shallow water, and this helps beaching. With the rudder lowered the effort of steering is reduced and the rudder acts more efficiently. The blade is raised by a laniard, and may fall under its own weight or be pulled down by a length of elastic shockcord.

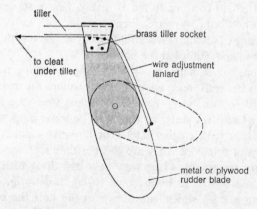

Figure 4 Rudder with lifting blade

Spars and Rigging

Sailing dinghy masts are usually of tubular aluminium or wooden built-up hollow construction these days, at least for the Bermudan rig which is almost universal in racing classes. They are quite slender, and are intended to withstand compression, with only limited bending. They are either stepped into a slot on top of the keel, with another support at deck level (or if there is no deck a thwart at gunwale level), or stepped on deck, with a post under the heel socket to take the stresses down to the keel. In the first case if the rigging parts the mast will probably break. In the second it will go over the side intact. In either case the mast is supported by shrouds and stays of wire rope, usually one shroud each side, and a forestay to the stemhead. The shrouds lead a little abaft the mast to support it against the pull of the forestay. The taller masts may also have diamond shrouds going round spreaders. In the case of small dinghies with only a simple lugsail or other basic rig, the mast may be solid and without shrouds or stays, although the halliard is then often led forward to act as a stay. I have successfully rigged an 8-foot (2·4-metre) yacht's tender with an unstayed mast made of aluminium scaffold tubing plugged with wood at the top and Tufnol at the bottom.

Rigging which supports spars is called standing rigging. The upper ends may be eyespliced round the mast, or shackled to fittings on the spar. Stainless steel wire is well worth its cost for standing rigging. The lower ends will be set up taut with rigging screws or laniards. Laniards are lashings of thin rope; they are cheaper than rigging screws, but have more give, which may be a bad thing with a tall mast, and are more bothersome to rig and unrig. When stepping a mast which goes down to the keel the rigging must be so adjusted that the spar floats centrally in its deck

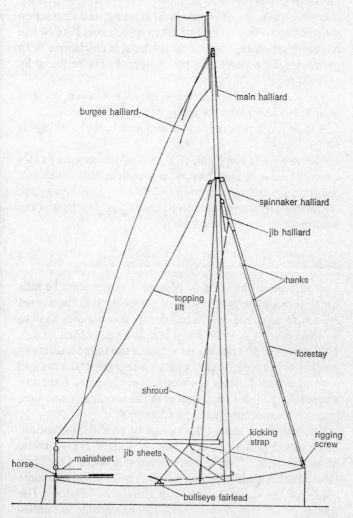

main halliard

burgee halliard

spinnaker halliard

jib halliard

hanks

topping
lift

forestay

shroud

kicking
strap

rigging
screw

horse

mainsheet

jib sheets

bullseye fairlead

Figure 5 Standing and running rigging of a dinghy

level support. It is best to set up the shrouds first, so that the mast inclines to the after side of its housing, and then set up the forestay to bring it central. The shrouds should of course be set up symmetrically so that the mast is amidships. With masts stepped on deck the best position has to be found by experience.

The other principal spar in a dinghy is the boom, which is attached to the mast by a fitting called a goose-neck.

A very large variety of mass-produced dinghy fittings is now sold, and most yacht chandlers have display panels or self-service racks for them. It is well worth acquiring catalogues of these fittings from makers such as Holt-Allen and Sea Sure, so that you can see what the various fittings are for, and what you can most successfully add to an existing boat or fit to one you are building.

Sails

The purpose of the mast is, of course, to support the sails which provide the propulsion for the boat. Sails themselves are not so simple as they seem, mainly because they have to set to a curve, to have flow as it is called, rather than set flat. This is achieved by cutting the edges of the sail to a carefully proportioned curve, so that when it is set against the straight edge of a spar fullness is thrown into the part of the sail where it is needed. I shall deal with the set of sails, and how it affects their performance, in Chapter 4.

Sailcloth used almost always to be made from cotton, preferably Egyptian cotton, but nowadays the synthetic fibres nylon and Terylene are invariably used. The name Dacron often mentioned as a sailcloth is the American trade name for the material known in Britain as Terylene. The synthetics are very strong, much less susceptible to mildew and other forms of decay, but their seams are rather more

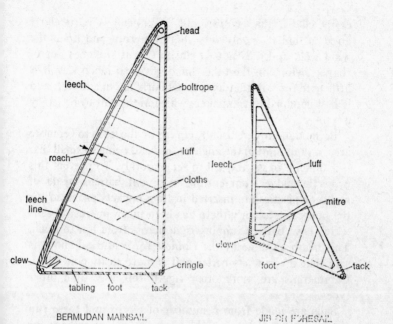

BERMUDAN MAINSAIL

JIB OR FORESAIL

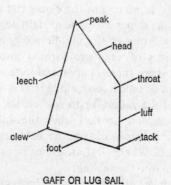

GAFF OR LUG SAIL

Figure 6 Sails and their parts

easily chafed than cotton sails'. Terylene is particularly good in that it is only very slightly porous and holds the wind well, and it is not so elastic that it stretches out of shape. Nylon, on the other hand, gives so much that it is little used for sails that have to set fairly flat in a breeze, and is best confined to spinnakers which are meant to be baggy anyway.

Bermudan sails are usually curved on the leech to get more area, and to prevent the angle at the head being so small that it is difficult to get the sail to set smoothly. To prevent this projecting edge from curling over, flat battens made of wood or plastics are inserted in long pockets provided for the purpose. Recently there has been much interest in sails which have battens running right across from luff to leech. This has been done by the Chinese for centuries, and it is said that the sail sets better and is more easily controlled. Catamarans are more often rigged this way than other types.

Sails are made from a number of cloths and these run either parallel to or at right angles to the after edge, or leech, of the sail. The latter is more usual, especially for Bermudan sails. In many jibs the cloths run at right angles to the leech in the upper part, and at right angles to the foot in the lower, meeting in the middle along a line called a mitre. The edges of sails are formed into hems called tablings, and where there is appreciable tension along the edge, a boltrope or tape is sewn along it. It is one of the most skilled tasks of the sailmaker to sew on the boltrope with just the right tension, so that when the sail stretches the strain remains properly distributed between the boltrope and the sail itself. Where all stretch must be prevented a wire luffrope is sewn into the tabling.

The very simplest of rigs sometimes have sails with a deep hem into which the mast slides, which eliminates the need for a halliard. Synthetic sailcloth is so strong that such small sails do not need much in the way of tabling, nor boltropes or reinforcement tapes.

At the corners of a larger sail the boltropes will be worked round a ring to form a cringle for the attachment of cordage, or some fitting. A jib would have its tack shackled down to a fitting on the stem head, a halliard shackled to the head cringle, and the sheets seized into the clew cringle. Sails may be attached to spars by lacings going through eyelets in the sail, or, what is more usual in present-day racing dinghies, the boltrope may run in a slot cut in the spar to a keyhole section, so that the rope cannot be pulled out directly, but can be slid out at the end of the spar. All these things vary in detail from boat to boat.

The setting and controlling of the sails is the function of the running rigging. The halliards hoist the sails, and run either through sheaves in the mast or through blocks attached to it. They are brought down to the deck, and made fast to cleats, or, in some cases, wound on to a winch. Wire is often used to eliminate stretch, but pre-stretched Terylene rope is more durable, kinder to the hands, and generally more satisfactory, at least for pottering. The sheets control the angle at which the sail sets, being attached to the clew, or boom end. They are usually of fibre rope, and often plaited line because it is kinder to the hands. The mainsheet will probably be in the form of a purchase, but the jib sheets will lead direct to a bullseye fairlead and to the crew's hand, although a snubbing winch or cleat may be fitted to make his work easier. One item of the rigging which comes in for more cursing than any other is the kicking strap fitted to many racing dinghies. This comes up from a point low down on the mast to a point some way along the boom, and its function is to prevent the boom lifting when the mainsheet is eased out. As it cuts across the place where the crew spends most of his time it is usually arranged so that it can be quickly detached from the boom. Its use does much to improve the set of a Bermudan mainsail.

Other parts of the rig are the spinnaker and its gear and I shall be dealing with these in Chapter 4.

Equipment

Any boat should have a good measure of independence of outside help, since it is part of the pleasure of sailing that one can go off on one's own, and to do this there are some other items of gear that should be aboard. A bailer is most important, as any sailing dinghy is bound to take water aboard occasionally, and there may be an occasion when you will be dependent on being able to bail to get your boat home. There should be a sponge to clear the last drops. Some means of propelling the boat in the total absence of wind is also necessary. In a racing dinghy this is usually a pair of paddles, but in a boat for cruising some distance a proper pair or oars with rowlocks is better, being much less tiring to use for a long period.

There may well be times when a foul tide with no wind makes it impossible to avoid drifting in the wrong direction if there is no anchor aboard. All that is needed is a folding anchor of the fisherman type weighing between 5 and 10 pounds (2·3 and 4·5 kilograms), or a little more for a really heavy dinghy, and perhaps 20 fathoms (37 metres) of 1½ inch (3·8 centimetre) warp. Even when racing, conditions sometimes arise where an anchor is needed.

Any loose gear in the boat, particularly if it will not float, should have a length of thin line spliced to it, with the end made fast to the boat. The bailer will not be much use after a capsize if it has sunk to the sea bed or drifted out of reach. On the other hand things should not be so securely lashed down that they cannot be released when wanted, whether the lashings are wet or dry. Elastic shockcord, which can be bought with hooks already fitted, is very useful for this purpose.

This book is not concerned with motor craft, but you may well think it a good thing to have some means of getting you home on schedule after a long trip, without too much exertion, in which case an outboard motor is the answer. The smallest outboards develop about $1\frac{1}{2}$ hp. There is no point in having a large outboard on a dinghy which is intended to sail. The British Seagull outboard takes a lot of beating for value and reliability, and is very easy to look after.

If you have to keep your boat afloat you will need a mooring for her, and it is as well to make this up yourself so that you know what the tackle is like. For most dinghies a single chain with a concrete clump is adequate. The clump should be about a hundredweight (50 kilograms), and cylindrical or mushroom shaped, with a strong eye cast in. To this shackle a length of $\frac{1}{4}$ inch (0·63 centimetre) chain; this should be about twice as long as the depth of water at high-water spring tides. Black chain is adequate for moorings which are under water all the time, but in these small sizes the extra cost of galvanized will be worth it because it is so much cleaner to handle.

The chain can itself be supported by a buoy, but where the tide runs strongly the weight of chain combined with the pull of the stream may pull the buoy under just when you want it most, so it is best to have a length of light rope spliced to the chain, and the buoy made fast to that.

Laying the mooring may be a messy job, and handling the heavy clump in your own dinghy would not be wise unless it were very heavy and stable, so it is best to borrow or hire a heavy boat for the purpose. In many anchorages there is a boatman who lays most of the moorings, and he will do the job from his own boat. It may be that the spot you have in mind uncovers at low-water springs; in fact this is no bad thing for a dinghy's mooring since it reduces congestion in the anchorage, and enables you to dig your mooring clump well into the mud. In any case make sure that the site leaves room for the boat to swing without touching any other craft, and if the area is controlled by a harbourmaster be sure to consult him first.

If the boat is to be kept ashore in a dinghy park you will need a trolley to handle her. Dragging a boat about on shingle or concrete is hard work, and very bad for the planking. All that is needed is a pair of small wheels on a frame shaped to hold the bottom of the boat. If she has to be pulled any distance it will be much easier if there is a tubular frame long enough to project beyond the bow when the dinghy is balanced on the trolley, as you can then pull and keep her level at the same time, like a wheelbarrow. If there is a good concrete hard, quite small wheels with thin solid rubber tyres will serve, but if shingle or sand has to be surmounted, balloon tyres large enough to give plenty of ground clearance are a must. Inflatable boat rollers are available which are the best answer on some kinds of ground.

It is very desirable for an open boat to have some kind of cover to keep out rain and leaves. Woven canvas which breathes is best, and the cover should be a good fit so that it does not blow undone. It can either go over the boom, or have its own supports to keep it up and free of puddles.

Safety Items

The two main types of safety equipment a small boat should carry are lifejackets and some form of distress signal. The first keep you afloat if you fall overboard from the boat (or while getting in or out of her) or if she capsizes. The second enables you to summon help if you really need it.

True lifejackets are made to a British Standard which calls for a great deal of buoyancy, aimed at keeping an unconscious person up the right way with his face clear of the water even when it is quite rough. This can only be achieved by having a large volume which makes the jacket bulky and inconvenient or worse for sailing. Most lifejackets are in practice inflatable, and can be worn partly inflated, but it may not be easy to blow in the rest of the air for full inflation after you have fallen in.

The alternative is the buoyancy aid, usually in the form of a jacket padded with plastics foam or other buoyant material, to give enough buoyancy to enable a conscious person to stay afloat without effort. These are what most people wear for dinghy sailing, and there is an approval scheme operated by the Ship and Boatbuilders' National Federation to endorse the design and construction of buoyancy aids, since they do not qualify for British Standard approval as lifejackets. Within their limitations buoyancy aids are perfectly satisfactory. A third type of personal buoyancy combines both functions, by incorporating buoyancy to SBBNF standards, with provision for inflation to provide enough extra buoyancy to meet BS requirements, and these are probably the best choice of all.

Young people should certainly wear at least buoyancy aids when sailing in open boats, and adults should too, except possibly in ideal conditions and close to the shore. They should in any case set an example to encourage children to wear them.

Many racing dinghy enthusiasts wear neoprene sponge wet-suits when sailing. These keep them warm, and provide buoyancy. However, they are not comfortable if worn for long periods, and would not be suitable for a day-long trip.

It is part of learning to sail to become independent of outside help (in fact, the feeling of independence is, I consider, one of the joys of sailing), and one should certainly avoid calling on rescue services unnecessarily. To do so puts other people to trouble and expense, and possibly danger, and distress calls made frivolously or because of gross incompetence reflect on all who sail for pleasure and increase pressures for legislation, licensing and control, things which we have so far been spared in Britain.

That being said, the small-boat sailor should carry with him the means of attracting attention in case of real need. The most usual signals are various forms of pyrotechnic flares and smoke markers. The recommended minimum for boats of less than 18 feet (5·5 metres) long is two distress signals, but a pack of three or more red flares and/or a mini-flare projector should be carried when going any distance from help (say out of shouting and waving distance, which means perhaps half a mile). Much depends on local conditions, both the natural features of the area, and the state of weather and tide. Remember weather can change quickly, so keep up to date with weather forecasts of the kind prepared for sailing people, whether the full shipping forecasts on Radio Two 1500 metres (200 kHz) long-wave, or local broadcasts. Clubs and harbour offices usually post up forecasts when they receive them.

Racing dinghies are normally accompanied by one or more rescue boats organized by the race committee and these should be able to cope with problems arising. Mostly they will be standing by when boats which have capsized are being righted by their crews. Because many racing boats are designed for speed rather than stability capsizes are common in squally weather, but this is taken as part of the game. For pottering the boat should be chosen to make a capsize unlikely, but if it does happen and the crew cannot cope as they should, they will have to call on the services of one of the rescue organizations, usually via the Coastguard. The actual rescue may be carried out by the Royal National Lifeboat Institution, Royal Navy or Royal Air Force helicopter, Coastguard, private rescue organization, or passing ship or yacht, depending on circumstances. I personally believe strongly that anyone who sails should be self-sufficient, aware of the limitations on his skill and endurance and keep within them, and know how to get out of trouble if he gets into it. He is then fit to set off alone, or with a chosen companion or two, within the capacity of his boat, and enjoy himself. Calling on the rescue services should be a last resort, but if it must be done it should not be left later than necessary. This calls for nice judgement.

3. How a Boat Sails

Anyone can see that a boat can blow along with the wind, but the fact that she can work her way in a direction as little as 45 degrees off the wind, so that by taking a zig-zag path she can progress into the wind's eye, needs rather more explanation. In fact an understanding of how this comes about is really necessary before the best can be got out of a modern boat even before the wind.

Wind Forces

The effect of hoisting sails into the stream of air which is the wind is to change the direction of the wind locally, and also to change its speed; in fact we bend the wind. In order to do this we have to apply a force to the wind, and as 'to every action there is an equal and opposite reaction' the wind comes back at us with a force which shows itself as a difference in the pressure on the two sides of our sail. This pressure difference can be thought of as a positive pressure on the windward side of the sail, although it is in fact made up of a positive pressure (that is a pressure higher than that of the air at a distance from the sail) on this side, and a negative pressure on the lee side: it is an observed fact that this negative pressure differs from the pressure at a distance by a greater amount than the positive pressure on the windward side of the sail.

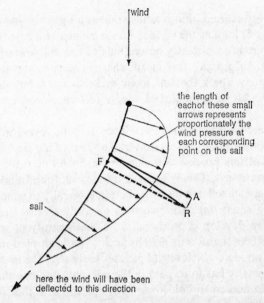

Figure 7 The forces exerted on a sail by the wind

However, thinking of the pressure as all being positive and on the windward side, it will act at each and every point of the sail at right angles to the surface at that point. As the sail is cut to set to a curve something like that shown in Fig. 7, and as it is also an observed fact that the pressure is greatest in the region near the luff of the sail, it follows that the sum of all the pressures at all the different points of the sail will act in the direction of the arrow A. As well as the pressure at right angles to the sail's surface there will be a much smaller friction force acting along the surface, the overall effect of which we will represent by the arrow F. These two forces combined give the resultant force on the sail, R.

This picture of things holds good as long as the sail is full, that is so long as the wind strikes it at such an angle that its pressure is consistently on one side of the sail, keeping it in shape. In practice this means that the part of the sail immediately abaft the luff must make a small but definite angle with the undisturbed wind direction, as shown in the drawing.

There has been a strong tendency over the years for boats' sails to get taller and narrower. The Bermudan rig was one stage of this process, but since it was introduced the trend has continued. This is because it has been found that for a given area a tall narrow sail is better, especially to windward, than a squat one. The reason is basically this: the force a sail can develop depends more on the quantity of wind it can deflect than on its area as such. A tall sail plan reaches wind up aloft which would pass uselessly over the lower rig. The penalty has to be paid in the tall spars and complicated rigging needed to hold these sails up, and in rather poorer performance when running.

How the Sail Drives the Boat

Now we can consider the boat in relation to the sail. In Fig. 8 the sail with its resultant force R is drawn with the outline of the hull beneath it, and you will see that in the position shown the resultant force acts in a direction at an angle to the fore-and-aft centreline of the hull of a little less than a right angle. As a result we can divide it up into two parts: a small force tending to push the boat ahead, P, and a considerably larger one, Q, tending to push it bodily sideways through the water. Now it is an essential characteristic of all boats intended to sail that they offer much greater resistance to being pushed sideways than ahead, so that the smaller force produces the larger effect. As a result

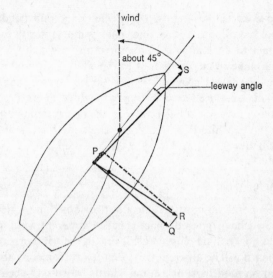

Figure 8 How the wind forces cause a boat to sail to windward

of all this the boat moves forward in a direction such as that of the arrow S, inclined at a small angle to the centre-line. This small angle is called the leeway, and the amount of leeway depends mainly on the shape of the hull, a large amount indicating one with an inadequate grip of the water.

Fig. 8 shows the sail set at an angle to the centreline which is about as small as it is profitable to use, and the boat would be said to be close-hauled. You will see that the boat's actual progress, arrow S, is at an angle of about 45 degrees to the undisturbed wind direction, and this is about the best that can be expected from any sailing boat. If the sail is pinned in further in an attempt to sail closer to the wind the direction of the resultant force R becomes so nearly at right angles to the centreline that leeway is greatly increased and forward speed falls off sharply.

Close-hauled sailing is, of course, only one condition among several, but it is the one which is most difficult for the beginner to understand. As the direction in which we want to sail makes a larger angle with the wind direction we can let out the sheets progressively, while still keeping the sails full. This has the effect of swinging the direction of R round so that it makes a smaller angle with the centreline, that is Q dwindles while P grows. As a result the boat is able to make better speed, with less leeway.

Apparent Wind

At this point we must take account of something which up till now I have ignored: what is called apparent wind. If we have a boat sailing close-hauled, Fig. 9, the wind experienced aboard will be different from that felt by someone aboard a boat on moorings, or ashore. This is because the boat, by moving through the water, sets up her own headwind; if she were a motor boat making six knots and there were no wind her crew would feel a six knot breeze from right ahead. As our sailing boat must have a wind to move in the first place, and as she cannot steer directly into the wind, she never experiences this wind from ahead, but it does seem that the wind is actually coming from a point further ahead than it really is. In Fig. 9 it is assumed that the boat is making four knots in the direction S, and that the wind, as felt by someone ashore, is fifteen knots from 45 degrees on the bow: the apparent wind will then be found by drawing a triangle to scale. In this case it amounts to eighteen knots from a point 36 degrees on the bow. This is the direction which will be indicated by the boat's burgee, and it may lead you to think that your boat is sailing closer to the wind than she really is. As, however, it is to the apparent wind that the sails must be set, the burgee gives a very good indication for this purpose.

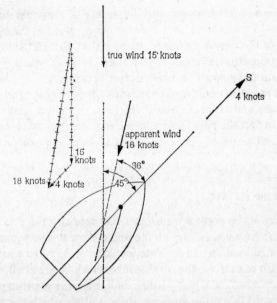

true wind 15 knots

S
4 knots

apparent wind
18 knots

36°

15 knots

18 knots 4 knots 45°

Figure 9 Showing how apparent wind differs from true wind

The same thing happens on all points of sailing, but whereas when close-hauled the apparent wind is always stronger than the true wind, when running free the reverse is the case, and the speed of many boats, particularly dinghies, is limited by the extent to which their forward speed reduces the apparent wind which acts on the sails. This is one reason why spinnakers are set before the wind, to increase the sail area. In the same way when we run before a breeze of some strength and then come on the wind we find the boat much more pressed, and may have to reef.

Another aspect of apparent wind is the fact that the apparent wind is fairer aloft. The friction between the moving air which is the wind and the surface of the water makes the wind speed less near the water. As the wind in the upper part of the sails is therefore stronger than that in the lower, the proportionate effect of the boat's forward speed is less here, and the apparent wind aloft is nearer to the true wind. As fore and aft sails tend to set with a twist, being nearest to the fore and aft centreline at the foot, this effect is allowed for; in fact the twist is usually greater than would be called for, and we usually try to reduce it as much as possible.

How the Fin Acts

Earlier in the book I mentioned the necessity for a sailing boat to have a good grip on the water. Now this is in practice obtained by doing under water something very like what we do with our sails in the wind. All boats which are at all good to windward have part of their hull, or some appendage to it, shaped like a fin, and just as the sail on which the wind blows obliquely develops a side force, the fin past which the water flows at an angle equal to the leeway develops a side force, and also a smaller friction force, as shown in Fig. 10.

It is a problem for the designer to provide enough area of fin. If there is too much the friction drag will be more than it need be. If too little the leeway angle needed to develop a side force which will balance that of the sails will be so great that progress to windward is slow, and also, because the fin is rigidly attached to the boat's hull, the boat as a whole is being dragged through the water at an angle, and so setting up more resistance.

We saw that with the sail the resultant force acted through a point much closer to the luff than to the leech, because the pressure was much greater in that region. In the same way the sideways force on the fin keel is not far back along it, but

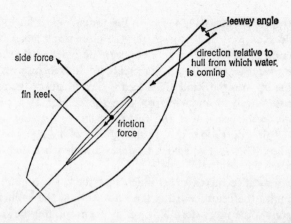

Figure 10 Forces on the hull due to its motion through the water

this is true only so long as the pressure is due to its movement through the water at a small angle. If we push the boat bodily sideways through the water, without letting her move appreciably ahead or astern, the sideways force developed will act at a point near the middle of the fin, but will tend to move to and fro in an unstable manner. This is important because it means that a boat sails much less controllably and with much more tendency to carry lee helm when she has little way on than when she is making good speed.

I remember seeing a good example of this on the Medway, where a Dragon class yacht was for some reason, probably defective reefing gear on the mainsail, beating up the river under a big genoa jib alone. She was sailing well, but when she was put about she lost a great deal of way, and as soon as the sail was full on the other tack her head blew round until she had the wind on her quarter. She then picked up speed again, and was brought back on the wind without difficulty.

In practice the boat's grip on the water owes a lot to the rudder as well as to the fin keel. For reasons which will become clear later all sailing boats are designed so that they carry weather helm, that is they tend, if left to themselves, to come up into the wind. This means that to steer a straight course the helmsman has to keep the rudder at a small angle to the centreline, and so to the fin, so that the combined fin and rudder can be thought of as a single curved surface. This sort of shape produces an adequate sideways force at a small leeway angle, although if it is carried too far the resistance increases so much that there is no gain. In dinghies the centreboard is the fin keel, and the rudder is usually some way astern of it, on the transom, but the same picture holds good. Dinghy rudders do tend to be larger in proportion to fin area than in other boats, and they make a useful contribution to the grip on the water when lined up truly on the centreline.

Points of Sailing

So far I have been describing in some detail the theory of sail and keel and how they propel a boat, and I have made use of a number of terms describing the different points of sailing. Now I must explain these terms, and give some idea of the ways a boat can be manoeuvred from one point of sailing to another.

Close-hauled sailing is, as I have said, sailing as near to the direction of the wind as it is practical to go, or about 45 degrees. If our destination is dead to windward we shall have to make a series of tacks or boards, and to change from one to the other we have to go about. This means to turn the boat so that the wind passes from one side of the sails to the other, the intermediate stage being with the boat head to wind and sails flapping like flags. If the wind is coming from

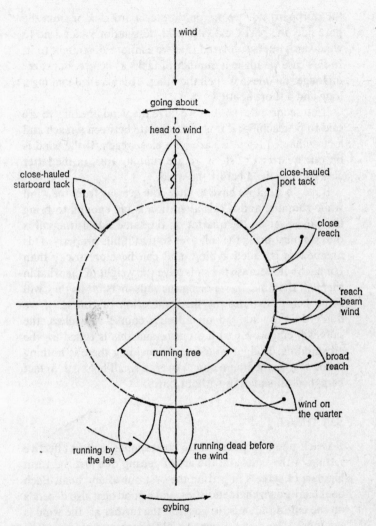

Figure 11 The different points of sailing

the starboard side we are on the starboard tack, if from the port side, the port tack. Often the destination is not dead to windward, but is so placed that we cannot sail straight to it. In this case we make a number of tacks as before, but carry on longer on one tack than the other. This is called making a long and a short board.

If our course lies so that we have the wind abeam, we are said to be reaching; if it is intermediate between a reach and a close-hauled fetch, we are on a close reach. If the wind is on our quarter or astern we are running free, in the latter case running dead before the wind.

It may be that we have to alter course away from the wind while running, and if this alteration is big enough to bring the wind over on the quarter on the same side as the sail is out, we must bring the sail over so that it fills properly. This manoeuvre is called gybing, and can be more tricky than going about, because the sails have the weight of the wind in them all the time, so we bring the sails in as far as they will come before making the final alteration of course. If we don't do this, and go on altering course regardless, the sails will come over with a crash, and this is called a gybe all standing. In light winds, and providing there is nothing in the way as the boom comes over, a small boat can in fact be gybed all standing without harm.

Sail Trimming

To each point of sailing there corresponds a most effective setting of the sails, and the art of getting this just right is a big part of success in getting the best out of any boat. Each boat has its own characteristics, and a good deal also depends on the cut of the sails. In general, the further aft the wind is the more sheet is paid out. An old rough and ready rule is that the boom, where a sail has a boom, or the line joining luff and leech where it has not, should bisect the angle between the wind and the boat's centreline. Thus a boat close-hauled with the apparent wind 30 degrees on the bow would set her boom at an angle of 15 degrees to the centreline, and

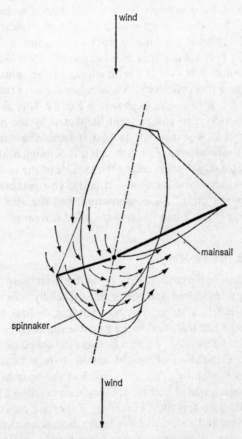

Figure 12 How spinnaker and mainsail interact to bend the wind when running

one running dead before would have it at right angles. However, I shall be dealing with the practical side of sail trimming in Chapter 4.

There is one important point, nevertheless, and that is that sails should not only make a bigger angle to the centreline when the boat is sailing free, but their shape should change so that they take a more rounded curve. Boomless sails, if properly sheeted, do this automatically, but a boomed mainsail, particularly if it is a tall narrow Bermudan one, will not and it is one of the functions of the spinnaker to make good this deficiency. A spinnaker is cut so that it sets almost in a semi-circle, as shown in Fig. 12. It is also set so that one side is to some extent blanketed by the mainsail, and when it is setting at its best it turns the wind back almost to the direction from which it is coming, at the same time increasing the flow along the lee side of the mainsail so that its efficiency is increased. It is this co-operation which gets the best out of the combination, and the idea that the spinnaker is just a bag to catch the wind is wrong.

Keeping Her Upright

The other important quality a sailing boat must have is stability; the force on the sails, especially when close-hauled, exerts a strong leverage tending to heel the boat over on to her side, and to be any use she must resist this. Stability is dependent on two factors: the shape of the hull, and the disposition of weight within it. In a boat of any size all the main weights are fixed, and the boat has to develop some angle of heel before they start exerting a righting force. They do this most effectively if they are concentrated low down, and so boats have heavy ballast on their keels. The dinghy, however, has one main weight which is very mobile, that is her crew, who may well amount to a sizable fraction of the whole weight of the boat under sailing conditions.

Dinghies therefore can normally dispense with ballast and rely on their crew to move about in the boat in such a way that she is kept upright. Apart from saving the weight and cost of quantities of lead or iron, the presence of this movable (and intelligent!) ballast makes it possible to keep a dinghy sailing upright under most conditions, so she can be designed to take advantage of this fact. Larger craft have to be very carefully designed so that they neither become much more difficult to push through the water nor more difficult to steer when heeled down, and this means some departure from the shapes which would be best purely from the speed point of view.

Because of not having to carry ballast, and because they can be made to a different shape, dinghies can, if they are light enough, be made to plane like a speedboat. This means that instead of being supported purely by the force of buoyancy, like any floating object, part of their weight is carried by pressure on the bottom set up by their motion through the water. In fact it is the old story of the sail in the wind and the fin keel in the water all over again, but acting upwards this time. For a boat to plane it must be light enough to be lifted appreciably out of the water by the dynamic forces, it must have plenty of sail area so that the necessary speed is set up in the first instance, and it must have been designed with planing in mind, because planing hulls have to have deep vee sections forward and a flat run aft.

When centreboard dinghies first became common it was generally thought that the plate had not only to be a retractable fin but also a retractable ballast keel, and it was made as heavy as it could be, usually being cut from steel plate, but in some cases being a massive iron or bronze casting. As dinghies became lighter, however, and the benefits of keeping a dinghy sailing upright became better understood, people began to realize that their centreboards were not in fact contributing much to the stability, and nowadays it is common to see them made of plywood, with just enough weight added to keep them down. There is one way in which a centreboard does add to a boat's stability, and that is by the resistance it exerts to being pushed sideways through the water. If something, such as a squall, or a rapid movement on the part of the crew, tends to make the boat roll, the centreboard is forced sideways through the water and slows down the rate of roll; it does not appreciably reduce the heel that the boat will take up under a given set of conditions.

Far from keeping the boat upright the centreboard can under some conditions tend to heel the boat. When sailing close-hauled in a fresh breeze it is the board which holds her up to the wind. If the board is raised suddenly the boat will skid sideways over the water, but usually at a reduced angle of heel.

When a boat is heeled the fact of the heel makes some difference to the way the wind flows over the sails, and to the way the water flows round the hull. In particular the air flows partly upwards as it goes across the sail, but this does not make any appreciable difference for practical purposes. One thing that does have a practical effect is that as the boat heels the area of sail exposed to the wind is effectively reduced, and a boat knocked down in a squall is in fact reducing the force producing the heel. A boat whose sails are almost parallel with the surface of the water will not have much wind pressure on them. In much the same way the centreboard becomes less effective as the angle of heel increases.

4. Boat Handling

Now we will suppose that the time has come for the first sail in your own boat. You run her down to the water's edge. If she is new or has been dry a long time she may leak badly at first if traditionally built, and in this case it is a good plan to leave her afloat half full of water overnight to swell the planking. If the leaking is of manageable proportions you can carry on with the sail, bailing now and again until the hull takes up. This 'taking up' is of course unnecessary with boats built of modern materials.

Assembling the Gear

With the boat afloat the first thing to do is to ship the rudder and tiller. The rudder may be heavy, with a metal plate, in which case it is very easy to drop it while working it on to its hangings. It is as well to see that there is a laniard to prevent this. The tiller should be fitted, usually under the mainsheet horse, and secured with a pin. If there is enough water it is not a bad idea to lower the centreboard, as it will steady the boat as you move around in her, and it will be ready for you to get away on any point of sailing as soon as you have set the sails.

Depending on conditions you will need to set either the mainsail or the jib first, but it is more likely to be the mainsail. If this has battens slide them into their pockets, making sure they go into the right ones if the lengths vary. Some pockets have a flap to prevent the batten from coming out, but many have a short length of thin line sewn in which is passed through two holes in the end of the batten, and the ends reef-knotted together. Others go in at an angle and drop into a pocket at the leech so they cannot fall out. Once the battens are in the sail handle it carefully, as it is easy to lean on a batten and break it.

Now attach the foot of the sail to the boom. I am assuming that your boat has the arrangement which is almost universal on modern Bermudan dinghies, but in others the principle will be the same, unless the sail is already laced to the boom in which case there is nothing to do here. You will find that the boltrope along the foot is brought out to the edge of the sail below the clew cringle. Push it into the wide part of the slot at the forward end of the boom and slide it aft. Feed in the sail at the forward end while pulling on the clew, which may have a length of thin line for the purpose. When nearly all the foot boltrope is in its groove push the tack cringle into the slot provided, and put in the pin which holds it in place. Alternatively there may be a lashing to secure the tack.

Next haul out the clew to the right tension, and make two or three turns with the clew lashing between the cringle and boom-end eye, and secure it with two or three half hitches. The tension needed will depend on the sails. The clew should be hauled out hand tight, just enough to prevent the foot from being baggy.

On racing dinghies there are often black bands marking the limits beyond which sails may not be hauled out, but this is to prevent people from setting more area than the rule allows, and is not an indication of where they should come to. As the sail stretches the slack must be taken up on the clew lashing, never using force.

The luff of the sail is treated in the same way. The halliard

Our own 8-ft (3 m) yacht's tender fitted out as simply as possible for sailing. Based on a grp hull moulding from Island Plastics of Ryde, Isle of Wight, she is carried on deck when we cruise in our 32-ft (10 m) sloop, and provides a pleasant way of exploring anchorages.

The essential minimum of gear for sailing — dagger board, rudder with tiller, mast and sail. This is our yacht's tender again. The sail has a pocket luff which the mast slips into, so there is no halliard, only tack downhaul, clew outhaul, and sheet. The mast, made from aluminium scaffold tubing, is unstayed.

One of a family of scows, variously prefixed West Solent, West Wight, and Lymington. Originally of wooden construction many now have hull shells of grp, like this one. They provide good sailing in sheltered waters, both racing and pottering. The simple standing lug rig makes them ideal for children and beginners generally, and they are responsive as well.

The Mirror dinghy, a chine design of just under 11-ft (3·5 m), intended primarily for amateur construction in plywood, has been built in large numbers. With a loose-footed gunter lug main and a jib of useful area, these boats give a good introduction to the sloop rig. The spars are short enough to stow easily. A good small dinghy for racing and pottering.

Two views of a 14-ft (4½ m) Leader-class double-chine ply dinghy illustrating how a boat of moderate racing type can have an exciting performance and will plane in the right conditions, while not being too extreme for a day's outing.

Top : Typical of the small, modern, grp racing dinghy, this Laser is the kind of boat you sit *on* rather than *in*. Fine for an hour or two's racing in sheltered water with rescue boats at hand, but with no claim to comfort or stability. Adequate for pottering.

In contrast here is a good-sized, partially decked dinghy with a generous freeboard, which serves very well for a day-long outing. Note the outboard, protected by a canvas cover, to get home with if the wind fails. She is, I believe, a Fairey Falcon, 16 ft 6 in. (5·3 m) long, and built by the excellent hot-moulded ply process, which is unfortunately no longer in production.

is shackled on to the head cringle or headboard, and the boom slid on to the goose-neck, making sure the foot of the sail is at the top of the boom. Most dinghy goose-necks have a squared part which makes it possible to reef by rolling the sail up around the boom and holding the turns by pushing it back over the squared part, but a new sail should never be reefed. While the boom is on the goose-neck, and the sail is not set, the end of the boom is liable to trail over the side, or get caught under the tiller, unless there is a topping lift, which is unusual in dinghies. The mainsheet purchase must be shackled to the boom end and the horse on the transom. The fall usually comes from the lower block on the horse, and should have a figure-of-eight knot in the end to prevent it from unreeving.

Now the sail can be hoisted. Make sure it goes up clear and does not foul anything. If you meet resistance don't force it but look and see what has fouled. The tension of the luff is determined in the same way as for the foot, but some sails have wire luff ropes, or wire as well as fibre ropes, so that the tension is set for you, and you can then set it up as hard as it will go. Jibs usually have wire luffs, and these too can be set up hard; in fact they must be for efficient sailing.

The jib will be shackled down to the stemhead fitting at the tack, and the halliard shackled to the head. It will probably also have clips called hanks to attach it to the forestay, and these must be snapped over the stay before the sail is hoisted. The jib sheets will have been rove through their bullseyes and the ends knotted with a figure-of-eight. All is now ready.

You are not likely to come across a true gaff sail in a dinghy, but you may have either a balance, standing or gunter lug. Standing and balance lugs are usually hoisted by a single halliard which is made fast to the yard about one third of its length from the forward end. The boom of a

c

Figure 13 Two ways of attaching the boom to the mast.

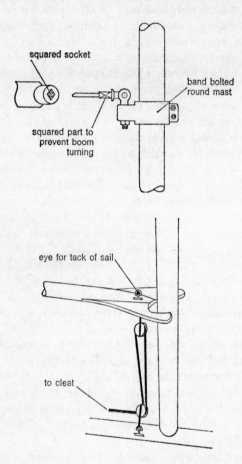

squared socket

band bolted
round mast

squared part to
prevent boom
turning

eye for tack of sail

to cleat

Above: a goose-neck, with provision for reefing the sail by
twisting the boom.
Below: jaws with a tack purchase. With this arrangement the
tension in the luff of the sail can be set up by bowsing down the
tack rather than with the halliard

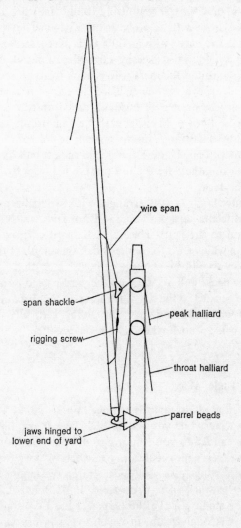

Figure 14 Rigging details of the sliding gunter

wire span

span shackle

peak halliard

rigging screw

throat halliard

parrel beads

jaws hinged to
lower end of yard

standing lug may be fitted to a goose-neck like a Bermudan one, or it may have a jaw fitting round the mast and then be tacked down with a purchase. On a balance lug the boom lies beside the mast, with again a tack purchase. Sometimes the yard is held to the mast by a traveller or parrel. A traveller is a ring round the mast with a hook for the strop on the yard, and an eye for the halliard. A parrel is a length of line round the mast with beads threaded on to it so that it slides up and down. In either case the halliard is attached to the yard by the fitting, and the sail can be hoisted, usually as high as it will go. If there is a goose-neck it will have to be set up hard. Otherwise the luff tension is put in by bowsing down the tack.

A gunter lug is usually arranged with two halliards. One is attached to the yard near the saddle or jaws which hold the lower end to the yard. The upper halliard is shackled to a wire span which runs for perhaps half the length of the yard. This span should be as tight as possible so that when the upper or peak halliard is set up the yard is held as nearly as possible parallel to the mast. Hauling on the throat or lower halliard will now send the yard sliding vertically upwards until it will go no further. The tack can then be set up as before.

Getting Under Way

It is best if at all possible to arrange things so that the boat is head to wind while you set the sails, and if you have done this you can let go your moorings and push her bow round on to the tack which will take you where you want to go. If you are starting from alongside a ramp or staging, arrange to be to leeward of it if possible. If the wind is blowing along the staging make the boat fast head to wind, unless there is a strong stream, in which case she will have to be

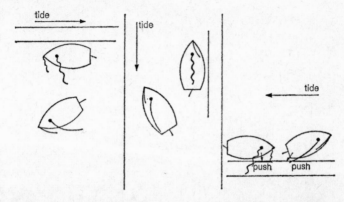

Figure 15 Getting away from alongside under different conditions

head to stream. Whenever you have to get away, as in this case, stern to wind, set the jib first, and get clear of your mooring under that sail alone, coming up to the wind when you can to set the main.

If you have to get away from a staging which is a lee shore, that is the wind is blowing on to it, set both sails, letting the mainsheet right out so that the sail flaps out over the stage, then push out from it with the paddle and sheet in quickly to get control. Stand by to fend off if she looks like touching either the stage again, or another boat secured alongside.

When you are starting from a mooring out in the river the same principles apply, but things are easier because you have a clear space round you to start with. With wind and stream together, set main and jib, drop your mooring, pay off on the tack you want, and you are sailing close-hauled. If wind and stream are opposed, set off under jib, head to stream, and come head to wind when opportunity offers to set the main. Lying head to tide with the wind abeam, the

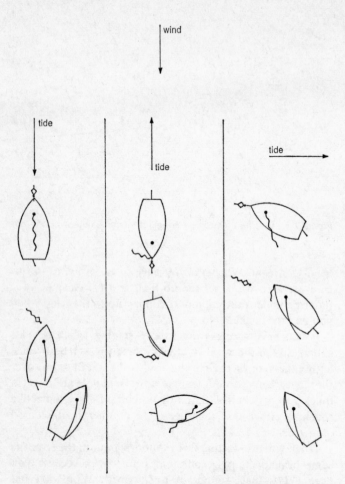

Figure 16 Stages in getting away from a mooring under different conditions of wind and tide

choice will depend on the relative strengths of the two elements.

Getting away from an open beach which is a lee shore can be a tricky business, as there will be some breakers coming in to complicate matters. The usual way is to set main and jib while the dinghy is on the beach, head to wind, and then get helpers to run her down into the water. It is a case of wading in, pushing the boat before you, scrambling in over the transom, and getting the boat under control as soon as possible. The main thing is to choose the tack which gives the more favourable slant for getting away from the beach. On some beaches it is usual to have moorings a little way off the shore, providing a means of hauling the boat out from the shallows.

Sailing the Boat

Now you are sailing the next thing is to trim the sheets to get the best out of the boat. If the sheets are paid out too far the sails will shake, and as a start you can let them just shake, then haul them in a little. It is more difficult to be sure that they are not pinned in too far, and it is necessary to cultivate a keen awareness of the wind direction relative to the boat. A burgee or racing flag at the masthead helps, and a length of ribbon half-way up each shroud is another useful guide. After a while you will find that you can tell a lot from the feel of the wind on your face and neck.

If you are sailing close-hauled you set the sails to the best position for performance on the wind, and then steer the boat so that they are kept full. The best position is found by experience, but a rough guide to start with is that the end of the boom should be over the lee gunwale aft, and the jib should be hauled in just about as hard as it will come, especially if there is any weight in the wind.

71

The first sign that you are sailing too close will be that the smooth curve of the jib's luff will become distorted by a bubble of wind playing on the wrong side. When this happens you will see the boat's speed fall off, and must pay off just a little.

If you are sailing too free you will see the burgee swing round to leeward, instead of being almost parallel with the boom, and the boat will be rampaging along, but not eating her way up to windward as she should. In most modern boats the jib overlaps the mainsail and you will sometimes find the wind from the jib blowing on to the lee side of the main, causing it to lift. This is wasteful, but if it is happening because the main has been eased out in a squall, it is better to keep the jib in since it is the more efficient sail.

You will sometimes see boats in a strong wind tearing along with their mainsheets paid right out and the sail flapping, but the jib still hauled right in. Sailing close-hauled in a responsive dinghy is a matter of nursing her along, and brings out the best in her helmsman.

Sitting Out

Apart from steering and trimming sheets the crew has to keep the boat upright. Although a dinghy will sail quite safely at a big angle of heel, resistance is much less, and steering easier, when she is upright, so to get the best out of her the crew must move their weight about to keep her as nearly upright as possible. In light winds this may mean only a slight movement out to weather, and it may even be more convenient for the helmsman to sit out on the weather rail, where he can see around him, while the crew sits to leeward to balance his weight. As the wind increases in force both will have to move out on to the weather rail, and lean further and further out until their bodies are horizontal and their tummy muscles are working overtime. There are normally straps along the centreboard case, or some other hold to catch your toes under.

Even when you cannot prevent the boat from heeling to some extent, your bodies should strictly be parallel with the surface of the water, doubled backwards over the rail, in order to get the best leverage. If the wind increases still further it is time to reduce the pressure by easing out the mainsheet, and if it is so strong that you have to do this continually it is time to reef, though few dinghies sail well reefed down. Sitting out is needed in strong winds on all points of sailing, except running dead before the wind. When the wind is gusty it calls for plenty of agility, as you have to move in sharply when the puff eases or the boat will lean to weather, which is unsightly and inefficient sailing. You may even capsize to windward, bringing the sails over on top of you.

Some dinghies are fitted with what might be called aids to sitting out. There is the sliding seat, a sort of plank running athwartships on rollers. The crew sits on the end of the plank and can rest his feet on the gunwale. By bending his knees he can adjust the leverage he exerts. It requires more agility in flukey weather and when going about than normal sitting out, but is less strain on the tummy muscles in a fresh breeze. In addition the crew can get his weight further outboard.

The other device is the trapeze. This is, as its name suggests, a belt or seat slung on a wire from a point up the mast. This contraption is only allowed in a few racing classes, and calls for a good deal of skill. The beginner is not likely to meet it. Its main purpose is to make it possible to hold the larger dinghies like the 505 and Flying Dutchman upright in fresh weather.

Trim

Apart from keeping the boat upright, you must make sure that her fore and aft trim is correct. A modern dinghy is designed so that the crew may be in their normal sailing positions and maintain the trim, but there has to be some adjustment for the conditions, and for the relative weight of helmsman and crew. A properly trimmed dinghy should have a clean wake, her transom just dipping below the surface of the water, and the wake streaming away smoothly without eddies or burbling. When she is moving fast there will probably be a plume of spray just abaft the rudder blade where the wakes from the two sides of the hull meet. If you move aft to look over the transom you will of course spoil the trim so you will have to judge from the wake further aft. If she is down by the head steering may be difficult, but this would suggest an extreme amount of bury. Again the wake is the best guide, since if the transom is too high it pulls up the water leaving the run, and a system of waves is set up in the wake. There will always be some undulation, but it should be as little as possible.

In the last resort judging the trim depends on experience of its effect on performance, and it is in these refinements of sailing technique that racing sharpens skill. When sailing close-hauled there is a certain amount of windage tending to push the mast and rig astern, which tends to lift the bow. When running there is a much more marked tendency for the bows to bury. As a result you will need to work your weight further aft when running.

A normally trimmed boat should tend to turn into the wind: this is what is meant by weather helm. Lee helm means that the boat tends to pay off, which can be dangerous as the sails then get fuller rather than tending to spill their wind. Any balanced boat should only carry a little helm when upright, and larger craft which have to sail much of the time at a considerable heel are designed so that they do not carry too much helm at any normal angle of heel. Dinghies are, as I have said, designed for maximum speed upright, and this is incompatible with balance when heeled. A hull of the normal dinghy form when heeled has a strong tendency to turn away from a side towards which she is heeled. It is in fact possible to steer a dinghy without a rudder by listing her first one way and then the other.

Moving about in a dinghy calls for some care even when you are not sailing, as it is quite easy to capsize a small boat by stepping in the wrong place. Your weight should be kept as far inboard as possible, and if you and your crew are both aboard you should keep on opposite sides of the boom.

Often you will have to go forward of the mast to attend to the mooring or shackle on the jib tack. When you do this you depress the bows, lifting the flat stable sections of the hull aft out of the water, and you may find the boat becomes very tender. If, as is the case in some small dinghies, it is not possible to get your weight far enough forward to do the job, get your crew to move right aft to keep the stern in the water. Bear in mind also that a lightly built racing dinghy will not stand up for long to heavy trampling, so move lightly, and keep your feet on the floorboards as far as possible. When sailing in light winds you will find that it pays to move about very gently as the slightest shock disturbs the flow of water round the hull and slightly increases the resistance.

Close-hauled Sailing

In the nature of things we spend more time tacking than on any other point of sailing, and although it is not the most spectacular condition it is the one which calls for most skill.

You must keep the boat moving well through the water, but not sagging away to leeward. Every little puff can be turned to advantage, because the momentary increase of wind brings the apparent wind a shade more free, and you can nurse her up to windward a little more without losing speed. You may be able to shoot up a little with the sails just on the shake, to ease her, but this depends on the weight of the boat and the windage of the rig. Modern dinghies, with their light hulls and tall rigs, have to be sailed all the time.

Sooner or later you will have to tack, and when you choose depends very much on the conditions. You may be in a narrow river or other channel where the length of the tacks is determined for you. In open water fairly long tacks are preferable, because you lose a little every time you go about, particularly in a strong wind and chop. If you are approaching a mark to windward your tacks should, for the very best chance of getting there in the shortest time, become shorter as you approach it, so that you work between two lines drawn at an angle from the mark. This evens out your chances of gaining or losing from a change in the wind direction. If the distance is not great, so that you decide to make just two tacks, you will find that you will need to carry on on the first tack until the mark comes just abaft the beam. If your boat sails more than 45 degrees off the wind you will have to go a little further still.

Going about itself has to be nicely judged if you are to lose as little way as possible in the process. If you put the helm hard down the rudder dragging through the water at a big angle will act as an effective brake. If you give too little helm the sails will be shaking for an unnecessarily long time, with the windage slowing the boat down. She should be eased round, but quickly as well as smoothly. Here again much depends on the boat and you will have to get to know her little ways.

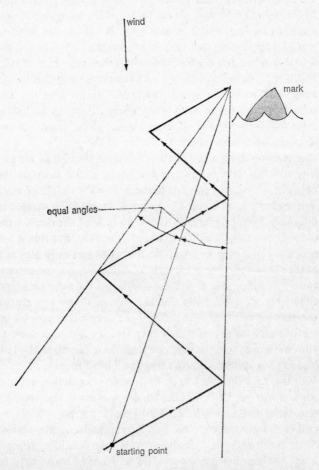

wind

mark

equal angles

starting point

Figure 17 If beating towards a mark to weather it pays to make tacks shorter as you approach it. In this way you are less likely to be put in an unfavourable position by a change of wind

The helmsman gives warning of his intention to go about by the command 'ready about' followed by 'lee-o' or 'helm's-a-lee' as he begins the manoeuvre. As she comes head to wind you and your crew will have to come inboard, and get ready to move out on to the new weather side. It is usually best for the helmsman to face aft as he crosses, so that he can keep hold of the tiller and mainsheet as he does so. The crew has the hardest time when going about, as he has to scramble across the centreboard case, while letting go one jib sheet and rounding in the other at the precise moment that she comes round. He should keep it sheeted so long as it is still full, but as soon as it is taken aback it should be brought across, and sheeted home before the weight of wind in it makes it hard work. Even a small dinghy's jib sheets can pull very hard in a breeze. If the jib is kept sheeted on the old side too long it will help to turn the bow, but this is not necessary in a responsive modern dinghy and only acts as a brake. It is even more important, however, not to sheet it over too soon, else it will fill aback on the new tack and effectively stop her from coming round. If for any reason she gets in irons, or misses stays, she may either pay off on the old tack again, in which case you try again as soon as you have way on, or she may make a sternboard. This means to go astern with the bows still head to wind.

In this case the thing to do is to remember that as soon as she has way on stern first the rudder will act in the opposite direction, and you will be able to make her pay off on the new tack by reversing the helm. Any modern dinghy should come about without difficulty provided she is sailing properly when the helm is put down. Old and heavy boats may be sluggish, and the best treatment here is to sail a little free for a short distance before tacking, so as to get up good speed, and then to ease her round firmly, holding on to the jib until she is properly round.

Reaching

Sailing on a reach after sailing close-hauled is like a holiday. The sheets are freed out and speed increases. Less exertion is needed to keep the boat upright, and she makes her best speed. Skill is concentrated on making sure the trim of the hull is just as it should be, and that the sails are trimmed to the very best advantage. Some boats may begin to plane on a reach, certainly on a broad reach. Only a light dinghy of racing type will really plane, but when it happens it is the most exhilarating thing that can happen in a dinghy. Trim is all-important in getting a boat planing. Some plane more easily than others, and there are innumerable variations suggested on ways to get her up. Some say you need a little wave to do it, others that you must move your weight aft, and then forward again. It is really a case of getting to know the boat, and advice from other owners in the same class may help you if you have difficulty. Planing ability depends basically on lots of power in the form of sail area, and as little weight as possible, combined with the right kind of hull shape.

Running

When the wind is nearly astern you may be disappointed in your boat's performance, because of the loss of strength in the apparent wind. As in reaching, trim and the set of the sails determine the performance. With the wind right astern you may find the boat beginning to roll rhythmically. This can be quite difficult to stop, and controlling it depends on anticipating the boat's movements so that you can counter them at exactly the right instant with your own weight. It may be affected by the amount of centreboard you have down. As soon as you are on a reach you can begin to reduce the amount of board, as the maximum lateral resistance is no longer needed, and raising it will reduce the wetted area, and so the resistance.

On a run you can in fact have the board right up, provided the boat has enough grip on the water to be steered adequately. In order to plane it is usually a good thing to have a little board down. If your course continues to call for paying off you will have to gybe. It is possible to run with the wind coming over the same quarter as the boom, this being called running by the lee, but this is to make most inefficient use of the sails, and can be quite dangerous in a strong breeze as it makes it very easy to gybe all standing.

To gybe in the normal way, haul in the main sheet as far as it will come, and bring the helm up until the boom goes over. Here the usual commands are 'stand by to gybe' and 'gybe-o'. Ease out the mainsheet as you move your weight over, and be prepared to stop her from running up into the wind. If there is not too much wind, and provided the boat has no runners or shrouds led aft, she can be gybed by leaving the sheet right out and swinging her round quickly so that the wind is almost abeam when the sail comes over. There will then be little pressure on it.

Spinnaker Work

There is not much to do with the jib until you are settled on the new course, because it will be blanketed by the main so long as you are running more or less dead before, unless it can be persuaded to stay out on the opposite side to the main to act as a small spinnaker, which is called 'goosewinging'. If you have a spinnaker, now is the time to set it. Spinnakers are usually symmetrical so that they can be set on either gybe without turning them round. The exact way of setting the sail will depend on how it is rigged, but there will be a

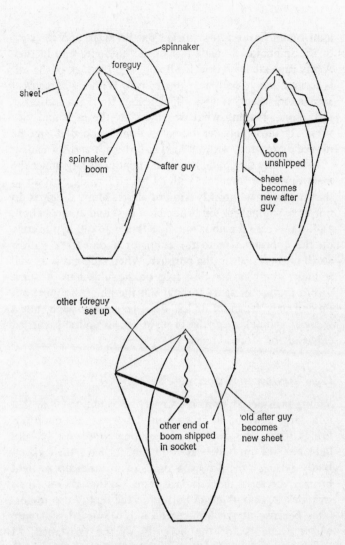

Figure 18 One way of rigging a symmetrical spinnaker, and how it is gybed

light boom fitting into a socket on the mast, and the clew of the spinnaker is made fast to the outboard end of this. A guy runs aft to control the boom, and the tack of the sail is secured somewhere near the lee rail. With a symmetrical spinnaker, when you gybe all you have to do is move the sail across, making what was the clew the tack and vice versa. If the spinnaker boom is double-ended it can be moved across too, without having to turn it end for end.

In a dinghy the spinnaker is best kept in its bag under the mast thwart or foredeck, with its halliard ready bent on so that it can be set quickly without effort. Many dinghies do not have spinnakers, on grounds of cost and complication, and in this case the jib is usually either held out by the crew on the opposite side to the main, or boomed out with a small pole carried for the purpose. When racing it is as well to make sure what the class rules on the subject are, as some forbid the use of spars to hold out the jib. A boomed out jib can only set more or less dead before the wind, but a well-cut spinnaker can be brought round and still carried efficiently on a broad reach.

Light Weather Sailing

Sailing provides an immense variety of conditions, and that is a large part of its attraction. Each set of conditions brings with it its own set of handling problems. In very light airs the most delicate adjustments have their effect. Badly setting sails are even more of a handicap in light breezes, because there is less wind to smooth out their wrinkles. A smooth clean bottom to the hull is also important, because at the low speeds it is frictional resistance which accounts for the majority of the resistance. At higher speeds its effect is swamped by that of wave-making.

One dodge which illustrates this is the deliberate heeling

down of a dinghy in light airs. This brings the curved bilge sections into the water, and lifts out the flat bottom part, so that the weight of the boat is supported at the expense of a smaller wetted surface, and hence the frictional resistance is less. Of course the resulting underwater shape is very different from what a boat's normally should be, but this only affects wave-making, which is negligible at very low speeds. The effectiveness of this dodge depends to some extent on the hull form of the particular boat, being most pronounced where there is a flat floor and a rounded bilge. Some boats have a vee section which would make it difficult to achieve much reduction in wetted surface, and chine boats will not respond so well either.

Freshening Conditions

As the breeze increases to moderate, less attention has to be paid to the more delicate adjustments of helm, sheets, and movement of crew, but things still have to be done right. It becomes important to keep the boat upright, because as the speed increases the effects of frictional resistance are swamped by those of wave-making resistance; hulls of dinghy form offer least resistance when upright because in this position they tend to set up the least marked wave system. As wind increases still further, more of the crew's attention becomes centred on keeping the boat upright, sitting out and playing the sheets as necessary.

Reefing

Eventually it will become necessary to reef. Most modern dinghies reef their mainsails by rolling the foot round the boom. The boom is slid a little way off the goose-neck, clear of the squared part, and then twisted so as to roll the sail round it. The leech must be kept pulled aft to prevent wrinkles being rolled in which would spoil the set of the sail. The halliard must of course be eased out at the same time. See that the luff rope winds in a neat spiral without bunching. When the area is reduced enough, and quite a small reduction can have a marked effect, the boom is slid forward again over the squared part of the goose-neck fitting, and the halliard set up taut again or the tack bowsed down as the case may be. Bermudan dinghies tend not to sail well with too little canvas, especially to windward, because the windage of the mast comes to have a dominating effect over the thrust of the sails. Going about may be difficult too as the windage can stop the boat before her momentum can carry her round. This is when it pays to have a heavy crew, to keep her upright and add to the momentum.

On a knockabout dinghy you may find the traditional reefing gear with cringles and points. With this there are one or more rows of lengths of thin line sewn into the sail along lines parallel to the foot, with a cringle worked into the boltrope on luff and leech. To reef you pull down the leech cringle of the reef you want to tuck in to the boom, and lash it there with a piece of thin line. Then do the same for the luff cringle. Finally roll up or fold the bight of the foot of the sail below the reef points and tie the two ends of each point together, with a reef knot of course, between the foot boltrope and the boom, not around the boom. The main thing is that the strain should never come on the points when the cringles are not lashed down. Where the sail has more than one row of reef points and cringles and you want to pull down more than one reef, it is sound practice to tie the first reef first, then the second, and so on, so that they can be shaken out one at a time as the wind moderates again. This traditional method of reefing can just as well be applied to boomless sails, and some foresails are fitted with points too. An alternative to reef points is a row of eyelets in the sail through which a continuous lacing, or individual pieces of line, can be passed.

Slightly larger craft often have roller reefing which is just the same in principle as that which I have already described, but the rotation of the boom is done by a worm gear or system of ratchets and a lever.

If She Goes Over

Capsizing is a thing that often happens in a light racing dinghy, and it can happen to any dinghy. It is not to be dreaded, and is as much in the day's work as falling off a horse is among riding people. However it is to be avoided if possible, because you will get very wet and it is bound to delay you, and in a race will probably put you out of the running.

The first line of defence against a capsize is sitting out and nimble adjustments as the wind force varies. As the boat is knocked down in a squall there is time to ease out the mainsheet so that she does not go right over. A light displacement dinghy with a deck and built-in buoyancy will lift as she heels, and go over to a remarkable angle before much water comes into the boat. Some become almost uncontrollable, because the rudder is lifted partly out of the water, and they run up into the wind and reduce pressure that way, but the sails then flog badly. If the squall is so fierce that she is still going over, it is usually possible to get out and put your weight on the centreboard, which will by now be lifting out of the water, to bring leverage to bear to bring her back. This requires quick action but it can be done.

Sometimes, however, you will not be able to prevent her from going over so far that she fills with water. She will now

85

probably be lying with the mast and sails more or less on the surface of the water, or just under it, and you and your crew will be holding on to the boat, or swimming round her. It is best to stand by the boat and get her up yourselves, as even if rescue is forthcoming it may well do more damage to the boat than any normal capsize will. How the boat will be floating will depend on the adequacy of her buoyancy, but she should be a good deal better than awash, provided you do not try to keep dry by climbing up on the hull. Although she should support you she will have negligible stability and it is best to resign yourself to swimming with just a steadying grip on the boat, while you set about getting her upright again.

It is usually best to get the mainsail down first, and this may be difficult with taut halliards. This is when you realize the importance of belaying them in a fashion which can be undone under any conditions. With the main down you and your crew can apply your weight so as to lever her upright again. It shouldn't need much effort, but the difficulty is getting her to stay upright, and not roll right over on top of you. It is best to be one each side to steady her, and then one of you can start bailing. As soon as possible one of you can get inboard and continue bailing until she will support you both again, when you can set off on your way under jib, and set the main if conditions permit.

The sort of things which make righting a swamped dinghy difficult are centreboard cases through which water can flow as fast as you can bail, and buoyancy arranged amidships so that the dinghy has no fore and aft stability and may at any moment put her stem or her transom in the air.

If a rescue boat does appear it is best to ask them to stand by while you right your boat, unless they are very experienced at the job and can help without risk of damaging boat or gear. A steadying hand on the mast can be a big help, and a motor pump to clear out the water also makes things easier. At all costs don't be persuaded to have your dinghy towed while full of water as this can do untold damage. In any case even quite a small motor launch along-side a dinghy in the sort of chop that is likely in capsizing weather can soon smash through the planking or carry away a spar.

Single-handed Sailing

So far I have been assuming that you have been sailing with a crew, as this is usual when racing most dinghies. Two-man races are by far the most common, and many people like to have a companion even when pottering. However there is no reason why you should not sail your dinghy single-handed. It is of course more difficult to sit a boat up in a breeze with only half the weight, but otherwise it is just a matter of getting organized to handle all the gear instead of only part of it. It is usual to fit dinghies which are going to be sailed single-handed with snubbing winches or jamb cleats for the jib sheets, but it is quite possible to hold both main and jib sheets in one hand. The jib sheet will lead across the boat from your 'forward' hand, while the main sheet fall runs aft to the horse, and by swinging your hand in an arc with either the jib sheet or the main sheet as a radius it is possible to adjust one without affecting the other. However the strain can be considerable if there is much wind. This leaves one hand free for the tiller. Any other adjustment, such as the centreboard, can only be done by letting something go, or cleating one of the sheets. Cleating the jib sheet is safe enough, but the mainsheet of a dinghy should never be belayed as a squall can so quickly capsize her if the sheet cannot be paid out smartly when it strikes.

Single-handed sailing will be more exciting in light or

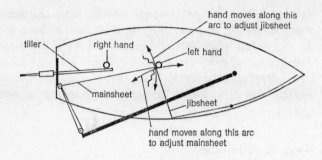

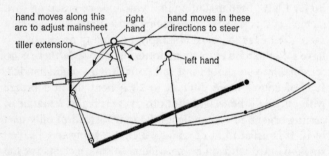

Figure 19 Two ways of sailing a dinghy single-handed. Minor adjustments can be made as shown; major ones will entail letting something go, or cleating a sheet, for a moment or two

moderate winds than sailing two up, but in strong winds the boat may prove too much of a handful.

Rule of the Road

Anyone who sets out upon the water should have a knowledge of the rule of the road at sea. The current version, which came into force during 1976, is a set of thirty-eight Rules and four Annexes. The Rules are given in full in

Reed's Nautical Almanac each year. The small sailing boat will be concerned mainly with Rule 12, which governs two sailing vessels meeting. This reads as follows:

'(a) When two sailing vessels are approaching one another, so as to involve a risk of collision, one of them shall keep out of the way of the other, as follows:

(*i*) when each has the wind on a different side, the vessel which has the wind on the port side shall keep out of the way of the other;

(*ii*) when both have the wind on the same side, the vessel which is to windward shall keep out of the way of the vessel which is to leeward;

(*iii*) if a vessel with the wind on the port side sees a vessel to windward and cannot determine with certainty whether the other vessel has the wind on the port or on the starboard side, she shall keep out of the way of the other.

(b) For the purposes of this rule the windward side shall be the side opposite to that on which the mainsail is carried or, in the case of a square-rigged vessel, the opposite to that on which the largest fore-and-aft sail is carried.'

For vessels under power the most important rules are that, when meeting head on each should alter course to starboard, and when crossing the one which has the other on her starboard side must give way. This last one is easily remembered as 'if you're on the right you're in the right'.

Other important rules state that power vessels must keep out of the way of sailing vessels, but that notwithstanding this any vessel overtaking another must keep clear. Small sailing craft must not expect large power vessels to give way to them in narrow waters.

The other rules govern lights and sound signals, what to do in fog, and distress signals.

The full rules should be studied by anyone taking a boat into open waters frequented by ships and yachts of some size.

Other rules apply between boats which are racing, but such boats should stick to the universal rules when near boats which are not racing. It is customary for yachts and other sailing pleasure craft to keep clear of boats which are racing, but this is a courtesy only and racing people have no right to insist on it. Boats racing are distinguished by having a square racing flag at the masthead instead of a triangular burgee. Boats not racing, if larger than dinghies, often wear their ensigns, whereas boats racing never do.

Bringing Up

When you have returned from a sail you will have to get back to your moorings, and you may well be suddenly struck by the thought that you do not know how to stop. In fact the only way to stop a sailing boat, short of bringing up with an anchor, is to remove the driving force, and allow her momentum to dissipate itself. The easiest way to do this is to turn head to wind, when the windage of sails and gear will help to slow you down. Even so it takes practice to know how far your boat will travel after you have luffed her head to wind. If you are coming to a mooring you may have tide to take into account as well as wind. If tide and wind are in the same direction it is easy as both will help you to stop, and it is just a matter of approaching from leeward, and luffing up before you get to your buoy. If you have judged it right the boat will come to a stop so that you can reach the buoy. If you overshoot you may still be able to reach out for it, but make sure you secure it quickly up forward, or the boat will be quickly swung round, the sails will fill, and you will probably be forced to let go.

If you have to approach a mooring with wind against tide it is best to lower the mainsail and run up to the buoy under jib, lowering this as soon as you have secured the buoy.

Much the same happens if you have to come alongside a staging or pontoon, or another boat. If it is possible to come alongside head to wind it is easy. If the wind is blowing directly off the stage you can come head to wind at right angles to it, judging it so that your boat loses way as she reaches it. You can go forward at the last moment to fend off and secure. As always the lee shore is the most difficult case, and here it is probably best to lower the sails before you reach it, and blow down slowly under bare poles, or get out the paddles.

Anchoring

If you have to anchor it is easier than picking up a mooring, in so far as the same degree of precision is not necessary. To anchor come head to tide, or wind if there is little or no tide, and stop the boat's way. When she is going astern over the ground, lower the anchor, paying out cable steadily so that it does not fall in a pile on top of the anchor. If you heave it all over at once it may foul on the upper fluke of the anchor, and prevent it from holding. With a fisherman type of anchor the amount of cable needed is at least three times the depth of water. Don't forget to allow for rise of tide if you are staying at anchor for any length of time.

Rope Work

An essential part of seamanship in any boat is the ability to do a few bends and hitches. The ones most used and most

Figure 20 Bends and hitches

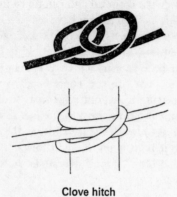

Clove hitch

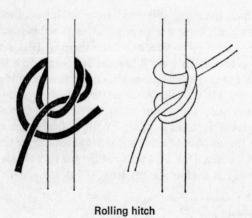

Rolling hitch

Reef knot

Sheet bend

Bowline

Round turn & two half hitches

useful are reef knot, sheet bend, bowline, clove hitch, rolling hitch, and round turn and two half hitches. These are best learnt with a length of line in your hands, and description is not a great deal of help, so the ways of making them are shown in Figure 20. Making fast to a cleat or pin so that the rope is secure but not jammed is also important.

Clothing

One other thing you may have been wondering about is what it is best to wear. There are always two schools of thought. Some people think that it is impossible to keep the wet out so it is not worth trying. These hardy spirits sail in shorts and sweater all the year round. It is true that in a dinghy you cannot wear the full equipment of oilskin jacket and trousers, with seaboots and sou'wester or hood, which are essential for keeping warm and dry in a cruiser in open water. However there are a number of waterproof smocks, jackets and trousers on the market which are quite light in weight. They should be made of fabric which is light, but tough enough to resist tearing, and should be coated or impregnated with pvc or synthetic rubber. Hoods are often fitted, but in sailing a dinghy are likely to be little used as a hood about your ears reduces that awareness of the conditions of wind which is essential if you are going to get the best out of a boat. It is as well to remember that, however warm it may be ashore, it is likely to be cooler out on open water, particularly if there is much breeze, and it is best to take a thick sweater.

Many dinghies send up a lot of spray, much of which goes over the crew, and if as much of it as possible can be kept from going down their necks, it is all to the good. A strip of towelling round the neck is a help. Full-length oilskin trousers may not be necessary, and may even be in the way,

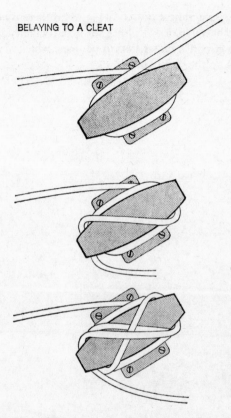

Figure 21 Start with a round turn. Then as many figure-of-eight turns as cleat will hold. End can be tucked under last crossing turn for extra security if needed, at risk of jamming

but short ones will make for comfort when you have to sit out on a side deck which on the last tack was intermittently under water. Canvas plimsolls are the only suitable shoes, and as feet are almost bound to get wet if there is any chop, socks are best avoided. Rubber soles, particularly if formed to give a grip, are better than rope ones, which absorb grit and mess up the paintwork.

The double-chine ply Wayfarer dinghy, a 16-footer (5 m), is big enough for dinghy cruising and also forms a racing class. Alternative sail plans are offered for the two roles, and grp hulls are also available. This boat is one of a number being used for instruction at a sailing school. The mainsail has been roller reefed as it was a squally day.

Unusual in many ways, this little boat is made of expanded polystyrene foam, and has long fixed bilge keels instead of a centreboard. The plastic hull is light, buoyant, and cheap, but will not stand much knocking about.

Best known of the Drascombe range of day-sailers is the 18 ft 9 in. (5·6 m) Lugger. She has a boomless lug main, leg-of-mutton mizzen, and a special well for the get-you-home outboard. A deep reef can be taken in the main using traditional reefing points.

The smaller Drascombe Dabber has many of the same characteristics as the Lugger, but she has a bowsprit. This one is going well on a windy day under jib and mizzen only.

Top : A keelboat with a shelter or cuddy forward, even if designed to race, can also be ideal for day-sailing in waters such as the Solent, where deepwater anchorages for larger cruisers are often overcrowded. The crew here are sensibly dressed for English spring weather! This boat is a 19-ft (6 m) Squib.

One of the most successful small production cruisers, the Westerly Centaur is 26 ft (8 m) long overall and has bilge keels which enable her to dry out upright and so explore shallow creeks. A thoroughly sensible boat which many owners have cruised in quite extensively. At least one has sailed across the Atlantic. This kind of boat will be many people's choice for a first real cruiser.

5. The Elements and Pilotage

As the wind is the sailing boat's source of power the more the sailing man can learn about how it works the better, both so that he can make the best use of it, and so that he will have some idea of when it is going to blow so hard as to make things difficult. This is not the place for a discourse on meteorology, nor would I be qualified to give one, but there are two things about the wind which are fundamental and which it is a help to understand.

The first is that most really strong winds in this country are caused by depressions, or troughs of low pressure which are usually associated with depressions. The second is that in fine weather in the summer, when there is in general not much wind, there is a tendency for the wind to blow off the sea on to the land in the afternoon, and from the land out over the sea at night. In the early morning and, especially, in the evening, the wind may well be very light. This can be a great nuisance when you are trying to get home in the evening after a day out sailing.

Wind and Weather

Nowadays the official weather forecasts broadcast by the BBC are much more reliable than they used to be, and the shipping forecasts, four times a day on the 1500-metre wavelength of Radio Two, give an excellent indication of what to expect. However, under many conditions the forecast is only true for a fairly short period ahead. They are usually for the next twenty-four hours, but the weather system can sometimes change unpredictably within twelve. The other thing to remember is that the areas are quite large, and there may be quite considerable variations within them. In particular around the coast each place has its own weather peculiarities and it pays to get to know them for your own home ground. Local forecasting offices will give you a good idea of what to expect in a specified small area over the telephone.

In the weather forecasts the strength of the wind is given in the 'Force' on the Beaufort scale. This runs from 0 to 12, calm to hurricane. Force 8 is a gale, the strength expected when gale warnings are issued. Boats, even dinghies, vary considerably in the amount of wind they can stand up to. Assuming sheltered water a dinghy should be reasonably happy up to Force 5; Force 6 would be about the limit for all but the sturdiest. However the amount of shelter provided by neighbouring trees and buildings has an important bearing on the matter. It is as well to remember that such shelter will reduce the average strength of the wind, but may result in its being made turbulent, with fierce eddies and gusts, which make sailing a very tricky business. On rivers especially the most freakish things can happen when it is blowing hard. I have seen boats running before the wind on opposite courses, and others almost becalmed while a few yards away crews are struggling to keep their craft upright.

Wind and Sea

If your sailing waters are at all open it will not be the wind force so much as the sea that will set a limit to what your boat can stand. The amount of chop which the wind can set up depends not only on the strength of the wind, but also on what is called the fetch. This means the distance the wind has travelled over unobstructed water, and so how much opportunity it has had to set up waves. In anything over a mile a gale of wind will set up a chop which will make a dinghy very wet to sail, assuming she will sail in so strong a wind, and the pounding might well damage her. Apart from the risk of damage to hull or gear, it becomes increasingly difficult to keep a dinghy free of water in such a chop, and if she does capsize it is much more difficult to right her. Exactly how much your boat will safely stand you will find out by experience, and you will probably find that it is more than you expected.

There is an old saying 'It's not the boats, it's the men in them', and it is true that most people are deterred by the discomfort before they reach a dangerous situation. This of course is provided they have not let themselves be caught by a sudden change in the weather while in an exposed place. It is for this reason that you should think carefully about the weather, and make sure you hear a forecast, before going out into the open sea in a small boat. In open water a small boat makes slow progress if conditions are unfavourable, and can soon tire her crew to the point where they cease to be able to cope intelligently with the situation. Although there is a good chance around our more populated coasts of being seen if you are in trouble, it is not right to put lifeboat crews and other helpers to the trouble and risk of coming to your assistance, through lack of foresight on your part.

Tides and their Prediction

The other element with which the sailing man is mainly concerned is the tide. Tides are set up by the gravitational attraction of the moon, and to a lesser extent by that of the sun, for the water of the sea, and consist basically of shallow waves travelling around the earth. The effect of this is that at any point there is a vertical movement of the water. The amount of this movement, and its timing, is greatly affected by the configuration of the coastline. The action of this vertical movement on shelving shores, and in estuaries and creeks, is to set up a horizontal flow in and out, and this is called a tidal stream. For our purposes the height of the tide will affect where we can sail, according to the available depth of water, and the rate and direction of the stream will govern our ability to make progress in any particular direction, for in our estuaries and around our coasts the streams are in many places strong enough to bring a small dinghy, sailing close-hauled, almost to a standstill, even if there is plenty of wind.

The time of high water in any particular place can be looked up in a tide table. These are to be found in the proprietary nautical almanacs like Reed's and Brown's, in the official Admiralty tables, and in many local newspapers and guidebooks. The main thing to remember is that they are usually made out for Greenwich Mean Time, and so one hour has to be added while summer time is in operation. You will find that the tides repeat themselves at intervals of a little over twelve hours, and in fact the time of high water works its way back to about the same time of day about once a fortnight, that is twice in a lunar month.

The height of the tide is by no means the same all the time. It also goes through a fortnightly cycle. Spring tides are the ones which come up highest and fall lowest, and neaps are those which have the smallest range, as it is called. Springs should theoretically occur when the sun, the moon and the earth are roughly in a straight line, but in fact they are two or three days after new and full moon in British waters. Neaps happen when the sun and moon make a rough right angle, after the first and last quarters. All spring tides are not of the same height, and the highest ones tend to be at the time of the spring and autumn equinoxes. The fuller tide tables give the predicted height of the tide for each day, the height being measured from the datum level of the charts, which in this country is normally Lowest Astronomical Tide (LAT), meaning the lowest level to which the sea is ever predicted to fall by astronomical calculation. It will only fall further still when exceptional weather conditions coincide with a very low tide. This is pretty rare.

To complicate matters still further, tides do not accurately follow the predictions as to height, and even as to time in some places, being much influenced by weather conditions. Strong winds tend to pile up the water on lee shores, and draw it away from weather shores, while the barometric pressure also has its influence. These variations tend to be more marked in the upper parts of estuaries and creeks, just where you may well be sailing your dinghy. In rivers the water level is of course also influenced by the amount of fresh water coming down from the upper reaches, and may well be appreciably higher after prolonged rain.

Tidal Streams

Tidal streams follow the times of high water, and the navigational publications such as charts, Pilots, and tidal stream atlases give the rate and direction for a number of points at various times before and after high water at some nearby reference port. In estuaries and creeks the tide naturally flows inwards as it rises and outwards as it falls, the direction changing at about high and low water, but with a tendency for the ebb to be stronger and more prolonged because of the influence of the fresh water coming down from the land. A useful tip, when you are working against a foul tide in a tidal river, creek or estuary, is that the stream is likely to be less strong, and turn fair sooner, along the shores than in the main body of the water.

Off an open coast tidal streams may turn at any stage of the tide, according to local peculiarities, change in direction half-way between high and low water being quite common. Here you will have to be guided by the published data, or by your own observations over a period of time. Here again local configurations of the land can cause large variations, and in some places the tide runs for as much as nine hours in one direction, and as little as three in the other. There may also be eddies.

The important thing to remember about tidal streams is that a little planning beforehand will enable you to get the stream to work for you, to take you out on your way out, and to help you back again later. Anywhere where the streams are at all strong, say more than two knots, trying to make progress against the stream will be slow and tedious work, and it is best to plan your time-table to fit the tides, or, if your times are fixed, to choose the direction in which you sail to make best use of the stream.

Where streams are strong, particularly round headlands, the water is often very disturbed. If the bottom over which the stream is running is also uneven, a race can result, and many of these races are no place for the small boat, especially if it is open. They are usually marked on the chart as 'overfalls' or 'ripples', and in heavy weather can give rise to a very nasty sea. In all such places where the streams run hard the conditions are worst when the wind and stream are in opposition, as the relative wind speed over the water is then greatest.

Basic Navigation

Most people sailing dinghies trouble very little about navigation, and the amount of importance you attach to it will depend on your chosen sailing waters, how far afield you go, and to what extent the art of navigation fascinates you. For me navigation has always been a pleasure in itself, and I have perhaps gone to unnecessary pains to fix my position on occasion, but there have been times when I have been very glad of having done so. Fog or rain can come down very quickly, and the inability to see where you are has a most demoralizing effect, even when it is not positively dangerous.

However, when sailing a small dinghy in clear weather there is little point in taking fixes or plotting courses, apart from the difficulty of handling charts and parallel rules in so small a boat. Unless the waters are really straightforward, however, it is as well to have a chart of them to study at home, even if you do not take it with you. This will show you where there are drying banks or rocks, and the position of buoys and other navigational marks.

Buoyage

Where there is a clearly defined channel, and even elsewhere, there is plenty of information to be got from a buoy, even if you have no chart. Buoys are laid out in accordance with what is called the Uniform System of Buoyage, with the Lateral System being the one usually found in British waters. In this system the most important thing to remember is that conical buoys, with a pointed top, which are usually painted plain black, or chequered with white, are intended to be left to starboard when you are approaching a harbour from seaward or are going with the main flood stream, that is the stream which flows while the tide is rising.

Conversely, can buoys, with flat tops, which are commonly painted red, either plain or with checked patterns of white, are to be left to port under the same conditions.

You will also come across round, spherical buoys which mark dangers which can be passed on either side, and buoys of all three types, painted green, which mark wrecks. The other main system, the Cardinal System, is much used in French waters. Details will be found in the Pilots and Reed's. A new international buoyage system, both simpler and more uniform than the existing one I have described, is to be introduced soon. Details of it, and of the planned times for its introduction, are now available in the standard references.

Until you are familiar with the various types of buoy they can be difficult to identify at a distance, as can buoys often taper towards the top, and may have lights or top marks on them which make them look pointed. This applies particularly to the larger buoys found in big ship channels, which are usually of a cage framework rather than solid. Another thing which may mislead is a buoy which at low water has so little weight of cable hanging from it that it leans over at an angle.

These buoys may either mark isolated dangers, or be arranged in lines on either side of a recognized channel. The question that arises is, how important is it for a dinghy to take notice of these marks? They are normally placed to mark water deep enough for sizable ships, usually not less than 3 fathoms (5·5 metres) at chart datum, although the smaller buoys may mark passages with as little as 1 to 2 fathoms (1·8 to 3·7 metres) in them, and in some places you find buoys marking channels which are dry at low water.

A dinghy, with its light draught if the centreboard is raised, can usually be got off fairly safely if she does ground, but with a fresh onshore wind it may be difficult to get her into deep enough water to be able to get the board down and sail her clear. Much will depend on the nature of the bottom. If it is softish mud it will be difficult and messy to get out and push her, and attempts to pole her off will only result in the pole sinking into the mud. On hard mud or sand it will be easier, but the risk of the boat being damaged by bumping in a choppy sea will be correspondingly greater.

Rocky shore should be given a wide berth, especially if there is any swell, as even if there does not seem to be much sea in open water, a foot or two of rise and fall on jagged rocks can make very disturbed water, and cause quite a lot of damage if the hull touches. Rocks tend to be steep too, and you may not have the warning that the centreboard provides by touching first on shelving shores. One compensating factor where the coast is rocky is that the water is often clear, and the danger can be seen through the water for a distance which may be adequate for a dinghy if the surface is calm enough.

In enclosed water, where there is not much likelihood of the sea getting up, and where the pleasure of dinghy sailing is being able to go where the larger craft cannot, there is little to be gained by following the marked channels. By working your tides so that there is the depth you want when and where you want it, and reconciling this with the stream directions if you can, you will be able to explore many places not easily accessible in any other way.

How Deep Will It Be?

It is useful to be able to work out what the depth of water is likely to be at various times between high and low water, and a fairly accurate estimate can be made by what is called the twelfths rule. This is that, starting from high water, the water will fall one-twelfth of its range in the first hour, two-twelfths (one-sixth) in the second hour, three-twelfths (one-quarter) in the third and fourth hours, two-twelfths in the fifth, and one-twelfth again in the sixth hour. This pattern repeats itself in reverse on the rising tide. The range on which to apply the rule will be found in the tide tables. Thus, if the tidal range is 15 feet (4·57 metres), one-twelfth is $1\frac{1}{4}$ feet (0·38 metres) and the depth two hours after high water will be $1+2=3$ twelfths, or $3\frac{3}{4}$ feet (1·14 metres) below high water; that is $11\frac{1}{4}$ feet (3·43 metres) above low-water level. Increasingly, now, heights are shown in metres. Note that the range is not the same as the height, which is what is normally shown in the tide tables. Height is the rise above chart datum on that tide. In some tables the height is given for low water as well as for high, so the range is the difference between these two heights. If the low-water height is not shown, the range is found by subtracting the mean tide level (from the almanac) from the height at high water, and doubling this difference.

The main thing to guard against when exploring unmarked waters in a dinghy is getting stranded on a falling tide somewhere where there is no water within reach for you to drag the boat to. It is quite possible to sail into a pool which is completely cut off at low water, and the main body of water may recede too far for you to be able to drag the boat to it. On any flat sand the water can drain off very fast and if you are not reconciled to the idea of sitting tight and waiting for the tide to return, it is as well to take special care when the tide is falling. If you go aground near high water and fail to get off you may have to wait nearly twelve hours for the tide to rise again. If it is just past spring tides the next tide may not come high enough to float your boat, and then will not do so for nearly a fortnight, but with a dinghy which is light enough to be dragged a short way you are almost certain to be able to get her down to the water on the next tide.

Navigation Instruments

The equipment you will need in a dinghy to apply the fundamentals of navigation is a chart, of the largest scale you can get, a compass, preferably so arranged that you can steer by it and take bearings, and some means of finding the depth of water, such as a short lead line, or a bamboo pole marked in feet or metres. The fullest range of charts is that published by the Admiralty, and obtainable from Admiralty chart agents. These are to be found in major ports only, but there are several in London, the principal one being J. D. Potter, in the Minories. There are charts specially prepared for the yachtsman by various publishers, notably Stanfords. These are usually on a smaller scale and combine more information on a single sheet. Personally I prefer to stick to the Admiralty series.

On inland waters, the upper reaches of creeks, and so on, you may well find that there is no chart, and here the best guide is an Ordnance Survey map. The 1/25000 series is very good, the sheets being small and easily handled, and the scale (about $2\frac{1}{2}$ inches to the mile) big enough to be useful. Mud banks and so on are marked on these maps, but they are not kept up to date with anything like the thoroughness of the true marine chart, particularly the Admiralty series which are always corrected up to the day of sale.

The purpose of a chart may seem obvious, but it is in fact twofold. It enables you to decide exactly where you are, which may not be as easy as it sounds, and it will then tell you in what direction you can go to get to your destination in safety. The simplest way to fix your position is to take two or more bearings with your compass of landmarks which are marked on the chart. If these bearings are then drawn as lines on the chart, the intersection of the lines will be your position. Now in a dinghy you will not be able conveniently to plot your bearings with pencil and rule, but having taken a rough bearing you can run your eye from the landmark shown on the chart, in the right direction, taken from the compass rose on the chart, and so get an accurate enough idea of where you are provided your marks are not too far away. In the same way you can see on the chart the direction you want to sail in, and look occasionally at your compass to make sure you are on roughly the right course.

A compass for taking bearings enables you to see the mark and the compass card at the same time, so you can make a note of the bearing while keeping the sight line on the mark. For steering, the compass needs to have a line or pointer called the lubber's line aligned with the centreline of the boat. Then if this lubber's line is opposite a certain point of the compass card, that point indicates the direction in which the boat is heading. It does not necessarily indicate the direction in which the boat is actually travelling, as she may be being set sideways by a stream, or be making leeway, or both.

Compasses suitable for small craft are available these days, the most important things being that they must be liquid filled, to keep the card steady, and be clearly graduated. A dinghy's compass will be best kept in a box, swinging in gimbals in the box if this is necessary (this will depend on how the card is pivoted in the compass bowl), and so arranged that it can sit on a thwart with its lubber's line properly lined up parallel with the centreline of the hull. It should be kept away from any massive ironwork such as the centreboard.

Finding Your Position

When sailing in unfamiliar waters it is very easy to lose track of exactly where you are, and it is the first principle of navigation to decide where it is that you are at regular intervals. Apart from taking bearings, as I explained above, there are many occasions when you can get an accurate position line, as it is called, by seeing that two objects, which must again be marked on your chart, are in line. They are then said to be in transit, and by projecting the line through the two objects as marked on the chart you have a very good idea of where you are. If you can find two sets of objects in transit, your position will be well and truly fixed. All this fixing of position is only really of importance when the waters on which you are sailing are of some extent, but even in a narrow river it is quite easy to lose track of the bends, which always seem to be much sharper than they are drawn on the chart because of foreshortening.

The real importance of knowing where you are becomes evident when you have to make a destination which you cannot see. This is of course what navigation in larger craft consists of all the time, but you may well find yourself in the position of having to do some real navigation in a dinghy if you occasionally venture out any distance from your base. Fog can come down very rapidly, and reduce visibility to a few yards.

One day you get stranded for a tide and have to find your way home in the dark, and our smaller creeks are not well provided with lights. If then you find yourself unable to see your destination, or indeed any point on the way to it, it will be a great comfort if you made sure that you knew at least roughly what your position on the chart was. You can then lay off a course in the right direction.

Accurate navigation depends, apart from using the compass, on some idea of the distance which you have travelled in a certain time. You will with experience come to know roughly how fast you are sailing through the water, and you will have some knowledge of the rate and direction of the tidal stream, so you can arrive at a rough idea of how far you have travelled after a certain time has elapsed since leaving your known position, or point of departure. It may be that there is some mark you can steer for which is sufficiently extensive to find without demanding great accuracy of navigation, but often the best thing for a dinghy will be to sail for shallow water along such a course that you know, when you touch bottom with your sounding pole or oar, or the centreboard if it comes to that, what bank it is that you have touched. It is then often possible, with the help of the chart, to feel your way along the edge of the bank, sounding often, to where you want to get to. Working in shallow water in this way you will also be unlikely to come into collision with larger craft in thick fog.

I hope I have said enough to show that pilotage of this sort is not very complicated, and that it can be great fun in itself. One day when things go wrong you may also find that a knowledge of your position makes it possible to get out of an awkward corner, and any practice you get with small craft will stand you in good stead when you come to handle something larger and go further afield, as I hope you will.

6. Maintenance

Boats need maintenance if they are to stay safe and hold their value. The work of maintaining a small boat is not too demanding and can be enjoyable. Professional maintenance of boats of any size is beyond most people's means – or at least would be such a large part of the annual running costs as to put the whole activity of sailing into a different financial category. Most people prefer to have a larger boat and maintain it themselves rather than a smaller boat professionally maintained, given the same total outlay. Owner maintenance is also valuable in that it teaches you about every part of the boat so that you are aware of its condition, and know what to do if something goes wrong.

If your boat was new at the beginning of the season, maintenance proper will begin at the end of the season with laying up. Many racing dinghy enthusiasts race through most of the winter, but the short days and cold winds are a discouragement to pottering, and a majority of boat owners lay their craft up for at least the worst of the winter. This provides time to go over the boat at leisure and make sure all is ready for the coming season.

But to some extent maintenance goes on all the time, defects are spotted and put right, and the sooner the better. There is also the need to avoid unnecessary deterioration by such means as fitting a proper cover which does not flap and chafe, and chocking a dinghy's hull firmly clear of ground where damp may damage it.

Laying Up

The first problem is where to store the boat. If she can be kept under cover, in a shed or garage, work will be easier, and there will be less of it because the weather will not be doing its inevitable work of eating into gel coat, paint and varnish, and wood if it is unprotected. Ideally it is best to have your boat at home where you can work on her whenever the opportunity offers without having to make a journey, as like as not forgetting some essential tools. If you have no shed or garage available your boat can be put up on trestles in the garden and covered with a tarpaulin. Provided she is well covered she will not come to much harm, but it will be less easy to get at her to work, and the weather will hold up work much of the time. However she is stored it is important to see that she is supported fairly evenly along her length, so that she does not tend to be distorted. With a traditionally built wooden boat the drying out of the timber will cause a fair amount of movement anyway, and if the hull is subject to strains at the same time, permanent distortion is almost bound to result. If you cannot bring your boat home to store for the winter you may be able to find storage space at a club or boatyard.

Apart from the hull, all the gear needs to be stored and in due course checked over. Sails should be washed free of salt, else they will absorb moisture and will always be damp. When they are dry go over them carefully to see if any repairs are needed. If they are, the autumn is the best time to send them to a sailmaker for the work to be done. Minor sail repairs can be done at home, and I shall be giving some hints on how to do them.

Cordage too should be washed free of salt and stored dry. During the winter you will need to go over all the rigging to see what, if anything, needs renewal.

Synthetic fibre rope, particularly Terylene or other poly-ester fibre, is very durable – in fact it lasts indefinitely if not badly chafed and worn. Much of the original running rigging of my eleven-year-old cruiser is still in use and, apart from being rather grey from dirt and weather, is as good as new. So if your cordage is not of Terylene or its equivalent, it is wise to change it at the first opportunity.

Wire rope rigging is normally either stainless or galvanized. Stainless is used for most standing rigging and the necessary end fittings or eyes are best done professionally, using either one of the swaging processes or a sleeve or ferrule splice such as Talurit. Stainless steel sometimes suffers from fatigue or embrittlement and should be checked regularly – say once a year – for cracked strands. At the first sign of this kind of failure the wire should be renewed. Even so a life of ten years can reasonably be expected of stainless steel rigging.

Running rigging suffers from the repeated flexing as it runs over sheaves. Stainless steel may have a shorter life than galvanized in this application provided the galvanizing can be kept up by protecting it. Once galvanizing has gone the steel under the zinc will rust, and the fine wires will soon fail.

There are two schools of thought about preserving galvanized wire. One is that it should be painted with linseed oil (boiled) or varnish, to give a weather-resistant coating. The other recommends greasing with lanolin or mineral grease to lubricate and preserve. There is probably not much to choose between them, but for running wire it is a good thing to work grease in. If grease is dissolved in petrol and then brushed liberally on, it will be carried into the inner strands, and left there when the spirit evaporates.

For running rigging there is a good deal to be said for using Terylene throughout, including halliards. Pre-stretched Terylene only gives a little more than wire and lasts much longer. But it needs to be much thicker – 1¼-inch/ 3·2-centimetre circumference is about as small as can be handled if a hard pull is needed – and sheaves may be of the wrong size if the existing halliards are of wire.

Apart from Terylene, cordage is made of nylon, which gives elasticity, and other synthetics including various forms of polypropylene and polyethylene. The last two make floating ropes, which are an advantage from some points of view, but also have the snag that they are easily caught by a passing motor boat's propeller. Terylene and nylon are the strongest ropes, and they sink.

There are various rope constructions, the commonest being the traditional three-strand spiral, and various forms of plaited or braided line. Three-strand is strongest and has least stretch, while plaited line is more flexible, kinder to the hands, and less liable to kink. It is best to choose between types on the basis of advice in the makers' literature, as each make has detail variations.

Wire is usually made from six strands with a central core which may be fibre or wire, or of a single strand containing (usually) nineteen wires. The latter is used for standing rigging only as it is rather stiff.

Rigging can be made up by a boatyard or chandler, but splicing and whipping fibre rope is easy enough, and pleasant work, and most people like to do it themselves. I have more to say about how to do this below.

Rigging Work

The first constructive work you are likely to be able to tackle is the overhaul of rigging, blocks, and sails. Rigging work will consist mainly of whipping ropes' ends to stop them fraying, either to replace old loose whippings or on new gear, and splicing in eyes.

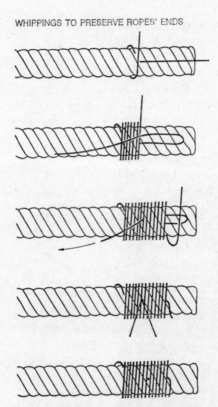

WHIPPINGS TO PRESERVE ROPES' ENDS

Figure 22a Plain whipping. Can also be done with a spike under the second half turns instead of the looped end of twine

The two best whippings are the sailmaker's and the plain, and as it is difficult to describe how to do rope work I have left it to the illustrations (Figure 22) to show how these are made. Personally I always like to use a sailmaker's whipping at the end of a rope and then put on an ordinary plain

115

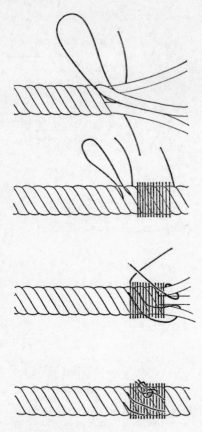

Figure 22b Sailmaker's whipping. Can be made without unlaying rope's end if needle is used to sew through rope between strands

whipping a few inches further up the rope in case the one at the end comes adrift. Whippings should not be made of twine that is too thick. Waxed Terylene is sold in various thicknesses and serves well.

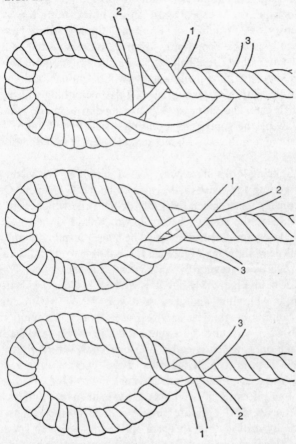

Figure 23 Sketches show first three tucks. Each unlaid strand goes under a different laid-up strand. Tucks are made in order as numbered. Eye is turned over to make tuck 3. Each unlaid strand is tucked in turn over one strand and under the next until each has been tucked four or five times (in synthetic rope). Ends are then cut off and melted

Instead of whipping you can buy plastic sleeves which can be shrunk on to ropes' ends. This is quick, but a less satisfactory way of doing the job than whipping, in my view.

All synthetic rope fibres will melt and fusing the ends in the flame of a match helps to make a whipping more secure. On very small line melting alone will be enough, although I would still prefer a whipping as well on anything which gets much use. The sailmaker's whipping can be made without unlaying the rope's end by using a needle and palm. This method, combined with melting, also serves well on braided line.

Splicing looks more complicated than it is. The secret lies in getting the twist in the strands to work for you. On a properly made splice the parts of the rope which were the inside of the strands before it was unlaid should still be inside on the finished splice. The stages in making an eye-splice are shown in Figure 23. It is possible to stop the end of a rope from fraying by what is called a backsplice. This is shown in Figure 24, but it is at best a clumsy substitute for a whipping, and may well jam if you try to run it through a block. The only real use for it is as a temporary job when you have no twine handy, in which case the first stage only, which is called a crown knot, serves almost as well. It pays to melt the ends of the separate strands after each one has been given its last tuck in any kind of splice.

Eyesplices are of two kinds, those made over thimbles and soft eyes. Soft eyes are simple enough as the size is not usually critical, but to get a splice to sit tightly round a thimble is not so easy. Paradoxically enough the best way is to make a soft eye which is appreciably smaller than the thimble over which it is to go and then force it over the thimble, stretching it as necessary with a tapered piece of wood, the proper tool being a kind of wooden spike called a fid. The ends of the tucks of an eyesplice are often served

Figure 24 Crown knot and backsplice

over, and a serving will also tighten an eye which is slack round a thimble.

Serving means binding over with twine, and usually goes with worming and parcelling.

Worming is filling the grooves between the strands of the rope with twine or marline, and parcelling is binding over with a protective covering of tape or strips of canvas. Worming is not worth bothering about on small rope, and parcelling can be quickly and conveniently done with insulating tape. It should be applied with the lay, that is it should spiral in the same direction as the strands of the rope.

Serving is done against the lay, that is of course spiralling in the opposite sense to the strands. When it is a splice that is being served, the lay against which it is applied is that of the part into which the tucks were made. The reason for this, and for the direction of all serving, is that the service then tends to prevent any untwisting of the rope strands, and so helps to lengthen their life, while any untwisting of the strands under load will tighten the service.

119

Serving is done with a mallet or board to haul it taut. To finish a service make the last dozen or so turns round the rope and round a short length of stick or rod laid along the rope. A spike or screwdriver will do. Pull the rod out, leaving a loop on each turn. Push the end of the marline back through these loops, and then pull each turn tight, using a spike as a lever, until you come to the end. Then pull the slack through with the end you pushed back through the loops, and cut it off short.

Blocks and Fittings

Blocks, and most other fittings for small boats, are today factory-made items manufactured in durable plastics, stainless steel, bronze, and other long-lasting materials. Maintenance consists mainly of keeping things clean, and lubrication where metal parts move on each other, as in swivels, screw threads, metal sheaves on metal pins, and the like. Most plastics run indefinitely on polished metal without lubrication or attention.

Where one metal fitting bears hard on another and lubrication is impracticable, as with a shackle pin in an eyebolt, wear may take place, so such points need to be watched and the worn part replaced when it is seriously wasted. Shackle pins should have their screw threads dipped in heavy grease, or better still anhydrous lanolin, so that they can be set up tightly and still come undone when necessary. This is especially important with galvanized shackles which, being much the cheapest, still have many uses.

Shackles which perform vital functions out of sight, as at the masthead of a cruiser, should be wired as an added precaution against their coming undone accidentally. Soft stainless steel wire, obtainable on reels from chandlers, is best for this. The end of a short piece of the wire is passed through the hole in the head of the shackle pin, through the shackle itself between pin and bow, and the two ends twisted together securely, but not so hard as to break the wire. Tuck the sharp end in where it will not catch on things.

Many modern fittings have loose pins with flat heads drilled across the other end for a split cotter pin. It is a good idea to keep spares for these clevis pins, as they are called, and for the split pins. I prefer brass split pins to stainless as they are not so hard and are easier to remove. They are strong enough for most purposes.

Tools used in connection with fittings include a spike (for shackle pins), shackle key (for the same purpose – a combined spike and key is convenient), and pliers. An adjustable spanner is often useful, and a hammer for tapping out jammed pins.

Sail Repairs

Repairs to sails will consist of making good any tears, holes, and chafed patches. Chafe along the boltropes is quite common, especially when the boltrope runs in a track, and this is probably best left to a sailmaker, but small tears are quite easily repaired using the herringbone stitch. For dinghy sails it is not necessary to use a sailmaker's needle, which may be difficult to get in the small size needed, and a palm will not really be needed either. The stitch is formed by making stitches on alternate sides of the tear, always in the same direction. The result does not cause a ridge in the sail, nor does it pull at the canvas. Holes, if small, can be darned like a sock, or, if larger, cut out square and patched. The patching can be done in the same way as it would be in more domestic applications. In all sewing work on sails it is a mistake to use thread which is too thick. Dinghy sails are not made of heavy canvas, and the thread to sew them should be about the same thickness as the threads from which the canvas is woven.

Temporary repairs can be made with sticky tape, preferably of the type sold for the purpose. Properly done they will last quite well. Extensive re-sewing of sails can be done by hand if time is unlimited, but a machine helps enormously. A zig-zag stitch is best, as it gives when the sail stretches. With the stiffer Terylene canvas now used for cruiser sails chafed stitching is one of the commonest forms of wear, and some re-sewing may well be needed before the material itself becomes too old and brittle to be relied on.

The Hull

A wood boat's paintwork is a very important part of its protection from weather and water, and needs to be carefully done. To take new paint or varnish, the surface must be clean, smooth, and preferably not glossy. This is best achieved by thorough rubbing down with waterproof sandpaper. Detergent or sugar soap in the water is a help. When the dusty mud which this will produce has been sluiced off with clean fresh water and the surface has dried, go over it to fill any cracks, dents, or chafed patches.

This should be done with a good quality stopping, not ordinary putty. Stopping can be bought in a variety of grades for application by brush, for fine cracks, or by a knife for larger defects. Ordinary stoppings rely on the drying out of solvents to harden, and can usually only be applied to a limited thickness else they do not harden right through. They have therefore to be applied in layers. Fillers based on synthetic resins can be applied to any thickness as they harden by an internal chemical process. They are at first sight rather expensive, as they are sold by weight, but they are not nearly as heavy for a given volume as stoppings based on white lead, and as it is a volume that you have to fill, it will be found that there is little to choose between them. The synthetics are in practice much more convenient and now used almost exclusively. Whatever type of filler you use it is likely to need rubbing down smooth when it is hard, and this is again best done wet with waterproof sandpaper.

There is now a wide range of marine finishes on the market, but the choice rests mainly between conventional paint or enamel, which dry by the evaporation of solvents and oils, and synthetic materials which set hard by the chemical action of polymerization. On wood conventional materials are as good as any, and are less fussy about weather and working conditions than synthetics. The best synthetic two-pot polyurethane sets so hard that natural movement in timber can cause their adhesion to fail. Variations in the moisture content of timber can also lead to synthetics lifting.

On grp (or aluminium alloy), however, the synthetics are undoubtedly the best choice, but it is a waste of expensive materials to apply them without proper preparation and strict observance of the makers' recommendations as to methods and working conditions. The details which follow are general recommendations for conventional enamels used on wood. The makers of synthetics issue very full instructions with the materials.

If a surface is to be re-painted it must now have an under-coat. Although some modern enamels have great opacity, undercoat is still needed as, apart from providing a background of the right colour, undercoat is of a thicker consistency than enamel, and will fill hair cracks and porous patches which were not amenable to stopping. You should bear this in mind when applying the undercoat, working it well into any joints or seams where the old paint has cracked. The surface of the dry undercoat may still not be perfectly

123

smooth, because of insects or grit or defects overlooked earlier, and if so it should be lightly rubbed down, again with waterproof sandpaper. If you really want to make a well-finished job, this process of a coat of undercoat followed by a rub down can go on for several coats until you are quite satisfied with the surface. Then the enamel can be applied. With a good surface this can go on thinly, and the main object is to avoid getting dust and insects on the surface.

For a varnished surface the principles are the same, but all the coats are of varnish, and each must, when hard, be rubbed down to a satin matt surface before applying the next coat. Cleanliness is even more important with varnish, since it is transparent. It is almost impossible to apply too many coats of varnish. It should of course be a true marine or yacht varnish, and be applied as thinly as possible. Three coats is a minimum on bare wood, and for a really good finish such as racing enthusiasts love, seven is quite a usual number. The final coat can be applied rather more freely than the others, to give a rich gloss.

If the old paint or varnish is in poor condition it will have to be stripped down to the bare wood. Paint is best removed with a blowlamp, but as this leaves scorch marks on the wood it is best to use a chemical stripper for varnish. The chemical has to be washed away or killed in accordance with the makers' instructions before new varnish can be applied. Really sharp scrapers are essential for good work, and care is necessary if the wood is not to be scored by the corner digging in.

With some timbers you have to take care which way the grain goes so that it does not lift under the blade. Teak is the easiest timber to deal with and will always scrape up bright even when long neglected. Softwoods are more difficult, and the surface tends to shred. In any case wood which has been scraped clean, whether dry, with chemical stripper, or by burning, will need to be thoroughly rubbed down, and here it is best to use dry sandpaper. The waterproof kind is more expensive, but if you cannot be sure of keeping it in a dry place it is better than the ordinary type, which is ruined by damp, even if you are going to use it dry.

Once the surface is free of old paint or varnish the work is much as described before. The first coat will be of priming for painted work, and it is a good idea to thin the first coat of varnish with a little turpentine or white spirit so that it soaks well in. If a synthetic resin filler is being used it is best applied to the bare wood, but if the ordinary solvent type it should go on after the priming. Undercoat can then be built up as before.

Where the boat is to be kept afloat in sea water the bottom will have to be painted with antifouling composition, otherwise weed and barnacles will grow in a few weeks in the summer. There are various qualities of antifouling which give protection for differing periods. The best are expensive, but a dinghy, which is easily beached for a scrub, can well make do with one of the cheaper ones. If the growth is not checked it will soon spoil the boat's performance, particularly to windward and in light winds.

Spars and Other Gear

Wood spars and various other items of gear will probably also need to be varnished, and here the treatment is much the same as for other varnished work. If spars need scraping down to the wood it is often as easy to scrape them dry with a really sharp scraper as to use chemical remover. The rounded surface makes it impossible to remove more than a narrow strip of varnish at a time and this does not need a great deal of force. The earlier the spars are varnished the better, as they are bound to have a good deal of rubbing from the rigging, and when they are being handled, so the varnish should be as hard as possible.

Aluminium alloy spars need little attention if anodized, apart from washing down. Bare aluminium will oxidize and will benefit from a few coats of two-pack polyurethane applied according to the makers' instructions.

Structural Repairs to the Hull

If at any time your boat gets damaged you may want to carry out repairs yourself. This is likely to be a good deal cheaper than getting a yard to do it, and adds to the satisfaction of ownership. There are many minor repairs which are likely to be done better by the owner, while for major ones the yard will have to be called in. Where to draw the line depends on your degree of skill.

Repairs to grp are not difficult and the methods are described in the literature of the material makers. The main types of repair needed are to superficial cracks and chips (in gel coat only), abrasion and structural damage. The first two require removal of dirt, debris and loose material, to leave a clean, and not shiny, surface which can be made good with polyester or epoxy filler. This will have to be cut down flush and smooth with abrasive paper when hard, and then polished. With structural damage one has to cut back to sound material and laminate in a new piece with glass fibre mat and/or cloth and resin, making sure everything possible is done to get good adhesion. After such a repair, if it is of appreciable size, it may well be worth coating the whole moulding with polyurethane to get a uniform finish.

The most likely repair to a plywood dinghy is patching with plywood which matches the original. To make a good job the damage should be cut out to a rectangle, and the edges feathered. A carefully fitted patch must then be made, with feathered edges also, so that there is effectively a scarph all round. The patch can then be bedded in glue and held in position with copper tacks well punched home. If some sort of clamp can be arranged to hold the patch in, so much the better. If necessary a backing piece can be added inside the hull to hold all secure, but this makes a clumsier job.

When all the rigging, painting, varnishing, and repairs have been done, fitting out will consist merely of re-assembling the gear and taking the boat down to her summer quarters. The work I have outlined may look formidable, but it will not normally be necessary to do anything like all the jobs in one year. It is worth making as good a job of these things as you can, however, because some of them affect your safety when sailing, and others help to make a boat keep its value as an investment.

7. Larger than a Dinghy

Most people who learn to sail in dinghies hope eventually to have something larger which will take them further afield, a cruising boat in fact. This is not a book about cruising or cruising boats, but it is possible to begin doing a little cruising even in a dinghy, and for little more than the cost of a large dinghy or dayboat it is possible to get a boat which with care will take you around our coasts when conditions are fair. This chapter gives some idea of the differences between dinghy sailing as ordinarily understood, and cruising.

Cruising in a Dinghy

If your dinghy is a substantial one, say a 14-footer (4·3 metre) with a moderate sail area and capable of carrying a fair amount of gear, there is no reason why you should not make coastal passages in her if you choose your time and place, and if she can be arranged so that you can sleep aboard. Alternatively you can have camping gear to sleep ashore. My preference would be for sleeping aboard; there may well be occasions when it is not easy to get ashore because there is only muddy landing.

A 14-footer (4·3 metre) should provide enough space for two people to lie down, one each side of the centreboard case. If the boat has a foredeck all that is needed is a fitted awning which will close round the mast and secure to the foredeck, and extend most of the length of the boat. If not, the cover will have to go round the stem too. The awning will be rigged over the boom, so some means for holding this up will be needed. You can either have a topping lift or a small crutch of some kind. The main thing is that the awning should be properly fitted and shaped so that it can be well lashed down. Screweyes or lacing hooks under the rubbing band make a good attachment. It is as well to see that the floor-boards are raised an inch or two off the hull shell so that there is room for a little bilge water, otherwise your bedding is bound to get wet sooner or later.

For sleeping in an open boat a sleeping bag is essential and some sort of cushioning under you very desirable. An inflatable beach mattress would be quite adequate, and less likely to get damp than any other sort.

The extent to which cruising in a dinghy is possible depends very much on the amount of open water which has to be crossed. While there have been dinghy races across the Channel, or at least Dover Strait, these have been organized affairs with numerous large craft in attendance to help out those who get into difficulties. For a beginner, I would say, it is unwise to try to cover more than ten miles of open sea in a dinghy, particularly if there are no intermediate landing places, and to do this distance it would be as well to have a leading wind. Frank Dye may have sailed to Iceland and other remote places in a sixteen-foot dinghy, but I would not recommend such trips to the inexperienced!

Plodding to windward in a chop is tiring in any sort of boat, but the smaller the boat the more tiring it is. In a dinghy there is no possibility of real shelter, nor can the boat be left to its own devices in safety as a decked boat often can, so if weather conditions worsen there is nothing for it but to carry on until shelter is reached. On certain parts of our coasts there are groups of harbours and landing places within easy reach of one another, and these are the places for dinghy cruising.

The Thames Estuary may have a nasty sea in it at times, but it is largely protected in southerly and westerly weather. There are many places a dinghy could call, from Margate along the north Kent shore, through the Swale with its tributary creeks, the Medway with the mass of creeks and saltings around its entrance, and across to Leigh or Southend when the weather is fair. It is then possible to get through into the Roach and Crouch rivers by the Havengore creek, and from the Crouch it is a short stretch round to the Blackwater via the Ray Sand Channel.

It would be possible to spend years exploring all these places in a dinghy, because a small boat can go up into creeks and inlets which are inaccessible to larger craft. Some are perfectly sheltered, while others are on a relatively open shore where it would be necessary to haul the boat out. It is the possibility of hauling out that makes it safe to cruise in appropriate waters with a dinghy, as, provided she is stoutly built and intelligently handled, it is only necessary to find a clear beach, without too much rock, and run her ashore when things look bad. It should preferably not be a lee shore of course, but even that should not be impossible of approach in the moderate weather which a dinghy should choose.

Another obvious cruising ground for small craft is the Solent area, where there are many charming, though now often crowded, harbours all within easy reach of one another. The Firths of Clyde and of Forth would also be suitable, and there are many other possible areas in British waters and elsewhere.

Not many people these days have unlimited time for pottering, and when sailing it is as well to remember that it may take longer to get back than it did to come out. It is a good idea to set off in a direction which will make the prevailing wind fair for the return, and to make as far as is wise as soon as possible, and then explore the harbours and anchorages as time permits on the way back. However it is always possible to leave a dinghy in some safe spot and travel home overland, to resume your exploration another time.

In the past it was quite usual to convert ships' lifeboats or naval whalers for cruising, with varying amounts of cabin accommodation. This was the cheapest way of becoming the owner of a boat of some size.

Suitable hulls are not easy to acquire now and a great deal of work is needed to make a reasonably sound conversion. Maintenance is likely to be demanding, too. Resale values of conversions also tend to be much less than for purpose-built boats.

There is no doubt that the best boat to buy as a sailing cruiser is one designed and built for the purpose. Bought new these will cost, according to size, specification and equipment, much the same as a car, ranging from the minimum cruiser for the cost of a family saloon, to a first-class 35 to 40 foot (10 to 12 metre) yacht at the price of a lavishly equipped Rolls-Royce.

There are many standard cruisers on the market, new and second-hand, but it requires a good deal of luck to buy at much less than the going price, so quite an investment will be involved. Perhaps the best value is to be had among boats of more than five years old which have been well looked after. Wooden boats much older than this (which may well not be of standard design) can be good value, but a professional survey, desirable for any second-hand boat, is vital for an older wooden one. As I have already said, good boats well maintained hold their value well, which will be an advantage when you come to sell.

As to what boat to choose, this will depend on so many personal preferences and other factors that it is impossible to give advice in a few words. But with some experience and much reading your own particular requirements will emerge of their own accord. In recent years the boats manufactured by Westerly Marine Construction Limited, Waterlooville, Hants., and Marine Construction (UK) Limited, Woolston, Southampton, have been among the most consistently successful. Both companies offer a comprehensive range of sailing cruisers.

Sailing the Larger Boat

As soon as you have to sail a boat of some size you discover the differences from dinghy sailing. Sitting out has little effect, and the boat has to be allowed to take up a fair angle of heel. She is more capable of looking after herself in a chop, and does not require such quick responses from the helmsman. On the other hand you have to take your navigation more seriously, as it is more difficult to get a larger craft off if she goes aground. You will also be confined to recognized harbours and anchorages as this size of boat cannot be hauled out on any beach, at any rate not without special tackle.

Sailing a decked boat in a seaway you learn how to work through the waves so as to get as little water aboard as possible. How to do this depends on the boat to a large extent, but the one universal rule is that if the boat is uncomfortable and hard pressed a reduction in speed will improve matters, especially when sailing to windward. All small cruising boats tend to be rather dumpy if they have any appreciable accommodation, and this prevents them from making good progress to windward in much sea. It is no use trying to drive on under a press of sail as the only result is to make the boat pound into the seas and stop her way.

Comfort Afloat

A boat with a deck and a cabin is an invitation to cruise more extensively than is possible in a dinghy, and it becomes more than ever necessary to consider home comforts. Your skill in handling the boat is the greatest single factor for safety, and skill is quickly undermined by inadequate food and sleep. Bunks below need not be elaborate, but to be any use at sea they should not be too wide, and should have some means of keeping the occupant in when the boat is heeled or rolling. A canvas leeboard lashed up to the cabin top is ideal. Even in some harbours you may find enough swell for these to be very welcome, and you may well want to sail at night.

Cooking afloat is most easily done on one of the portable appliances run off bottled gas – usually butane, sold under brand names such as Camping Gaz (widely available) and Calor Gas (UK only). This gas has its dangers when used in the confined spaces of a small boat's cabin but, with care and proper regard for recommended safety rules as to installation and use, can be safe enough. The simplest installation, with a gas cylinder mounted directly on the stove assembly, is probably the safest in a small cruiser. The traditional small boat cooker is the Primus, or other make burning vaporized paraffin, but these are now rather expensive, and in many cases more complicated to light than gas burners. Many cruising people still prefer them, however. The main thing is that it should be possible to heat up soup or hot drinks at sea if you are going to be out more than an hour or two, and make a good hot meal in harbour. To be any use at sea any stove must be swung, at least athwartships, so that the kettle or pan keeps upright. Gymbals can be bought for Primus stoves, but it is not a difficult job to make a swinging tray on which the stove can be mounted.

Food leads on to the question of seasickness. Few people are sick in dinghies. The motion is too quick, and there is no shortage of fresh air. In a cabin boat the motion is that much slower, and in a stuffy cabin one is much more liable to feel at least dizzy, and very probably really sick. People vary enormously in the extent to which they are affected, but if the motion is really violent there are very few people who are completely immune. There are drugs which are in varying degrees effective in preventing real sickness, but most of them have some unpleasant side effects, such as a dry mouth, drowsiness or depression. These things don't matter very much to the passenger in a big ship, but the crew of a small boat has to be alert and, although the early stages of seasickness are themselves debilitating, the normal person gets acclimatized after a day or so. Only experience can tell you whether it suits you better to take one of the recognized remedies, or to take a chance on what comes and hope that you will get acclimatized reasonably quickly. In any case you are not likely to be making very long passages in rough conditions in the sort of boat we are considering here.

Night Sailing

Sailing people often try to make their passages in daytime, and this may mean reaching harbour at or after dusk, when finding your way to a berth in an unknown place can be quite worrying. If you have to make a passage which is likely to take at least several hours there is a good deal to be said for sailing by night. If the coast is well provided with lights, navigation is in many ways easier by night than by day, particularly if you have a hand-bearing compass with an illuminated card. You are then likely to arrive in day-light, and should have no difficulty finding stores and provisions. In the summer, winds are often lighter and steadier at night too. If you do sail by night the important thing is to have really good navigation lights. In a small boat the electric ones with their own dry batteries are probably the best, especially for an occasional night at sea only. Not only must they be bright enough but they must be put somewhere where they can be clearly seen, and not obscured by the sails. Port and starboard lights, and a white stern light, are really necessary, also some means of illuminating the binnacle. The tricolour masthead light provided for in the new regulations is a great improvement, although it can really only be supplied from a proper electrical installation.

The main extra risk of night sailing is that of being run down by a big ship, and it is as well to have a powerful torch as well as the navigation lights, so that this can be shone on the sails or on some white part of the boat to call attention to your presence. There is a lot to be said for keeping clear of shipping lanes in a small boat at night, and one way to be sure of this is to keep in shallow water. Unfortunately most shallow water channels are only marked by unlit buoys. The other thing to remember is that if someone goes overboard it is very difficult indeed to pick them up again in the dark. I consider that anyone on deck at night in a small boat should wear a safety harness and some form of lifejacket. It is also possible to get small waterproof lamps to clip on to the lifejacket, so that it is much easier to find the man overboard in the dark. At least one lifebuoy with attached flashing light should be carried.

The other thing to remember about night sailing is that even in the summer nights at sea are very cold and a really adequate supply of woollens is essential as well as good oil-skins, which keep the wind out as well as the wet. Pvc or synthetic rubber coated oilskins are the best, and a suit consisting of short jacket and trousers will last for some years. The expensive coats with built-in harness and inflatable buoyancy are a great convenience.

Craft of this kind can give an immense amount of pleasure. There is nothing quite like arriving in your own craft under sail in some quiet anchorage as the sun sets, letting go the anchor and looking around you over the water, still in the evening lull of the breeze, and savouring the sense of achievement which is your right for having brought her there. At times there will be hard passages and you will begin to wonder whether you are really doing this for pleasure, but it is the joy of sailing that it provides so many different varieties of experience.

Crewing for Other People

When you have been sailing in dinghies for a year or two, and perhaps in a more sizable boat too, you may begin to feel you would like to sail in one of the larger and more famous craft which cruise far afield, or take part in the better-known ocean races. It is usually easy enough for someone with some knowledge of sailing to get a berth as crew in one of these yachts, particularly when racing. The best way to do this is through your own club, but if this does not have any ocean racing members, or members who own substantial cruisers, it may be worth joining a club further from home for the purpose. Competent and reliable crews are always in demand for races, as a really full crew is then needed, and owners are more likely to take someone they don't know because they will only be cooped up with them for a day or two. Getting a berth aboard a cruiser may be more difficult, as the wise cruising man knows that a crew member must not only be useful but also congenial and compatible as a companion if the cruise is not going to cease to be a pleasure for the whole ship's company. However, once you start sailing you become a member of a community and soon make friends with other like-minded people so it is not likely to be long before the opportunity of a berth arises.

Once you are a crew aboard someone else's boat it is as well to exercise a little tact. Above all remember the owner or whoever is in charge counts on having things done as he thinks fit, and it is up to you to do them that way even if you do not agree with his ideas. In all sailing boats, knowing the boat and her gear counts for more than knowing about sailing in general, and even such simple things as belaying a rope or hanging up a coiled fall may have to be done in a way which is unfamiliar to you. Racing yachts often have a quick turn-over of crews, and usually their gear is fairly standard, though of course very different from a dinghy's, but cruising boats are very often the expressions of their owner's individuality and it will take time to get to know how all the gear works. Racing has in a way a more limited objective, since it is to win that is the aim, but the motives of the cruising man are more complex and the amount of emphasis placed on achievement, or safety and comfort, will vary accordingly.

The other way of gaining knowledge and experience, which I have already mentioned briefly, is by the formal route of sailing schools and RYA qualifications. Now that a scheme has been set up which recognizes sailing experience, rather than being merely an adaptation of the examinations set for officers of big ships, it is well worth while to try for the RYA scheme qualifications, which culminate in the Yachtmaster's Certificates, coastal and offshore. It will pay to take recognized courses at schools based ashore and afloat to pass the various examinations. I would not go so far as to say that all who can sail competently and in safety will pass, nor are all who qualify fully capable all-round cruising skippers, but the scheme as a whole is an excellent one and well worth pursuing.

It is inevitable that any book on sailing should be to some extent a catalogue of pitfalls for the unwary, but no one is likely to be put off by this, especially as the hazards have very little reality when they are read off the printed page. It is not until you get out to sea and things begin to go wrong that some suggestion you have read may come to mind and prove useful. The main thing in learning about boats is to acquire that kind of sixth sense which comes to seamen, so that they feel uncomfortable about a set of conditions without really quite realizing why, and so are on their guard. This cannot be acquired by reading, but once you have been to sea the more you read of other people's experiences the more you will learn of the way the sea works. At sea, even if you are racing, the primary task is to gain the utmost advantage over the elements rather than over other people.

Books for Further Reading

The library of books on sailing is very extensive and new titles are constantly being added. Many books quickly become dated in these days of rapid change, and others are more entertaining than informative. The list which follows, a tiny selection, gives some of the enduring books and standard works I think sailing people can benefit from reading – and enjoy as well. I have also listed magazines, since I believe anyone who sails should take at least one regularly, if only to keep up to date with developments, which may be either technical or to do with rules and regulations at sea.

Eric C. Hiscock, *Cruising under Sail* and *Voyaging under Sail* (Oxford University Press)
The standard works by the greatest living authority. The first a comprehensive guide to coastal and cross-Channel cruising, especially useful for those with the older type of boat. The second extends to cover ocean passages – if it does not make you want to sell up and go far your heart's not in the right place for cruising! Eric and Susan Hiscock, the most famous of cruising couples, have three-and-a-bit circumnavigations of the world behind them, as I write in 1976.

Bruce Fraser, *At Home in Deep Waters* (Newnes)
One of the best of many general books on cruising to appear in recent years. An ideal introduction to sailing a reasonably modern boat.

Cours de Navigation des Glenans, Vols. 1 and 2 (Editions du Compas, Paris)
Vol. 1 covers basic sailing in dinghies and open boats, Vol. 2 cruising in larger boats. Probably the best current books on the subject but should be read in French: Vol. 1 only has been translated into English but I consider it has lost something in the process.

Mary Blewitt, *Navigation for Yachtsmen* (Iliffe/Stanford)
Thoroughly sound introduction to open water navigation.

Jeremy Howard-Williams, *Sails* (Adlard Coles)
Comprehensive standard work including setting, maintenance and repair.

Yves-Louis Pinaud, *Sailing from Start to Finish* (Adlard Coles)
The out-and-out racing man's approach to dinghy sailing – comprehensive, authoritative and lavishly illustrated.

Donald M. Street, *The Ocean Sailing Yacht* (David and Charles)
Faintly eccentric but thoroughly sound and readable advice on all aspects, especially as related to the larger, older boat.

Hervey Garrett Smith, *The Arts of the Sailor* (Van Nostrand Reinhold)
Rope and canvas work comprehensively covered in a delightful style.

Hervey Garrett Smith, *Boat Carpentry* (Van Nostrand Reinhold)
Woodwork afloat for fitting out, repair and maintenance, blending sound instruction with great charm.

Arthur Beiser, *The Proper Yacht* (Adlard Coles)
Design considerations and examples for the larger yacht –
quite recent but sure to become a classic.

Captain O. M. Watts (Ed.), *Reed's Nautical Almanac*
(Thomas Reed Publications)
The annual with full details of tides, movement of
heavenly bodies, and much essential reference material
besides.

The Mariner's Handbook (NP100, Hydrographer of the
Navy, HMSO)
Thoroughly professional on charts, pilotage and many
other aspects of the seaman's work. Those parts not
directly relevant to the pleasure sailor, e.g. navigation in
ice, have their own fascination.

Catalogue of Admiralty Charts, Home Edition (Hydrographer of the Navy, HMSO)
List of charts with key plans for British Isles and North-
West Europe – a cheap guide from which to choose charts
of your local waters.

Guy Cole, for the Department of Trade and Industry,
Safety on Small Craft (HMSO)
Good basic introduction with official backing.

Seaway Code (HMSO)
Elementary but thoroughly sound guidance from official
sources in a small booklet.

How Safe is Your Craft? (HMSO)
Basic recommendations in a government leaflet.

Safety in Outdoor Pursuits (HMSO)
Government booklet with a section on sailing which
gives some useful advice.

Admiralty Pilots and Pocket Tidal Stream Atlases for areas
of interest.

Many areas are also covered by privately published sailing
directions intended specifically for yachtsmen; these are
always useful, in some cases indispensable, but often expensive compared with official publications. Official publications
of all kinds are kept up to date and revised editions are
published whenever necessary.

Periodicals

Practical Boat Owner (Monthly)
Invaluable blend of information on all aspects of sailing
except racing, with a good deal on power craft, the
emphasis being on the handyman's approach. Read more
for information than entertainment.

Yachts and Yachting (Fortnightly)
Deals with racing and cruising, much about dinghies, and
has newsy items.

Yachting Monthly (Monthly)
Concentrates on cruising with an instructional bias but
also has some items more intended for leisure reading.

Yachting World (Monthly)
Emphasis on racing and 'up market' boats, good technical
articles from time to time and has an ear close to the
official side and the yachting 'establishment'.

Glossary

Abeam: in a direction at right angles to the boat's centreline.

Aloft: above deck level, in the rigging.

Anchor: a device which will hook itself into the sea bed and hold a boat stationary.

Apparent wind: the wind felt aboard a moving boat.

Apron: a member inside the stem to which the plank ends are fastened.

Athwartships: across the boat.

Awash: just level with the surface of the water.

Backstay: a stay supporting a mast against forward pulls.

Ballast: weight carried in the boat to increase stability.

Batten: a slat of wood or other material let into a sail to stiffen it.

Beam: the width of a boat; a thwartships member supporting a deck. *On the beam* means 'abeam'.

Bearing: the angle relative to north at which you see an object.

Beat: to progress to windward by tacking.

Belay: to secure a rope so that it can be released again.

Bend: to tie a rope to another rope or to a sail.

Bermudan rig: a rig with a triangular mainsail pointed at the head and with no spar at the head.

Bight: a loop of rope or fold of canvas.

Bilge: the lower part of the hull; the turn of the bilge is where the topsides blend into the bottom. *Bilge water:* water which has collected inside the boat.

Blanket: to obstruct the flow of wind to another boat or sail.

Block: a pulley through which ropes run.

Bollard: a device with two squat posts for belaying large ropes.

Boltrope: the rope sewn to the edge of a sail.

Boom: a spar running along the foot of a sail; any similarly rigged spar.

Bowse: to haul taut with a purchase.

Bullseye: a ring-shaped fitting without a sheave, through which ropes are run.

Buoy: a float which marks some object or supports a mooring.

Buoyancy: the force by which a floating object is supported. *Buoyancy tanks, cases, bags:* devices for providing buoyancy to dinghies otherwise full of water.

Burgee: a flag flown at the masthead, showing membership of a yacht club.

By the lee (to run): to run with the wind on the same side as the sail.

Capsize: to turn a boat over.

Carvel: built with planks butted edge to edge.

Catamaran: a boat with two narrow hulls held some way apart.

Centreboard: a flat fin lowered through the bottom of the boat to give a grip on the water. *Centreplate:* a metal centreboard. *Centreboard case:* the box which houses the centreboard and keeps the water out of the boat, which would otherwise come in through the slot.

Chafe: rubbing of gear or hull and the damage so caused.

Chine: an angle in a boat's hull, as where flat sides join flat bottom.

Chop: a short sea.

Cleat: a T-shaped device for belaying rope.

Clench: to rivet up a boat nail. *Clench-built:* clinker-built.

Clew: the lower after corner of a sail.

Close-hauled: sailing as close to the wind as is practicable.

Cloth: one piece of canvas in a sail.

Clump: a weight used as a mooring anchor.

Course: the direction in which the boat is pointing.

Cringle: a ring worked in the corner or boltrope of a sail.

Crown: the part of an anchor where the shank joins the flukes.

Daggerboard: a centreboard which is not pivoted but slides bodily downwards through the case.

Deck: a horizontal surface to walk on, or to keep the water out.

Deckhead: the underside of a deck.

Dinghy: a small, usually open, boat which may or may not have sails.

Draught: the depth of water a boat needs to float her.

Ebb: the tidal stream due to the falling tide.

Fair: favourable (of a wind); clear and unobstructed.

Fairlead: a device for guiding a rope so that it runs freely.

Fender: a softish pad to protect a boat against a quayside or other craft.

Fid: a wooden peg or spike.

Fix: to derive a position in navigation; a position so derived.

Flood: the tidal stream due to the rising tide.

Floor: a strong frame across the bottom of a boat; the bottom of a boat in general. *Floor-boards:* boards to walk on in a dinghy.

Flow: curvature in a sail.

Fluke: the arm of an anchor which bites into the ground.

Foot: the lower edge of a sail.

Fore-and-aft sails: sails whose luffs are secured on or near the centreline.

Forefoot: the curved part of the stem below the water where it joins the keel.

Forestay: the principal stay forward of the mast.

Forestaysail: sail set hanked to the forestay.

Frame: the member which runs athwartships across the planking, in this case usually of the solid grown kind.

Fray: to unravel (of a rope's end).

Free: sailing so that you are able to alter course without pinching or going about.

Freeboard: the height of the boat's side from water to gunwale.

Gaff: a spar supporting the head of a quadrilateral sail, and secured by jaws or otherwise to the mast.

Genoa: a large jib which overlaps the mainsail.

Go about: to bring the wind on to the other side of the sails via the head-to-wind position.

Goose-neck: a flexible joint between boom and mast.

Gudgeon: an eye forming part of the rudder hangings.

Gunter lug: a rig with a yard which runs up almost parallel with the mast.

Gunwale: the upper edge of the topsides; the stringer placed there.

Gybe: to bring the wind on the other side of the sails via the stern-to-wind position. One also says '*port gybe*' and '*starboard gybe*' as 'port tack' and 'starboard tack'.

Gymbals: devices consisting of pivoted rings to keep equipment horizontal when the boat rolls or heels.

Halliard: a line which hoists a sail or other piece of gear up the mast.

Hank: a clip used to hold a sail to a stay.

Headboard: a flat-shaped board fitted into the head of a Bermudan sail.

Headsail: any sail forward of the mast, or foremost mast if there is more than one.

Heel: the angle at which a boat leans over; the act of so leaning.

Helm: the tiller; the act of steering and being in charge, hence helmsman. *Weather helm:* a tendency to luff. *Lee helm:* a tendency to pay off.

Hitch: to tie a rope to a spar or fitting.

Horse: a bar along which a block slides.

Hull: the shell structure of the boat itself.

In irons: head to wind and out of control.

Inboard: within the boat.

Inwale: same as gunwale.

Jaws: a crutch-shaped device to hold one spar against another.

Jib: a headsail, usually set flying (i.e. not hanked to a stay); the outer headsail where there are two. Often used for the only sail forward of the mast whether it is strictly a staysail or not.

Keel: the structural member running along the bottom of the boat. *Fin keel:* that part of the hull which is fin-shaped to give a grip on the water. *Ballast keel:* ballast fixed to the keel so as to form part of the fin keel.

Keelson: the member lying on top of the keel, to which the garboard strake is usually fastened. It sometimes runs over the frames.

Kicking strap: a line running from under the boom to low down on the mast to prevent the boom from lifting.

Knee: a wooden bracket holding two parts of a boat together.

Knot: a speed of one nautical mile per hour.

Land: the overlap of one plank on another in clinker construction.

Laniard: a thin line which holds an item of gear; a lashing on the lower ends of shrouds and stays to adjust their tension.

Lay: the manner or direction of twist in which rope is made up from its strands.

Lead line: a line with a weight, marked at intervals, for finding out the depth of water.

Lee: away from, sheltered from the wind. *Lee shore:* a shore where the wind is blowing from the sea towards the land.

Leeboard: a hinged fin attached to the topsides to give lateral resistance when lowered; a board to keep a sleeper in his bunk when the boat is heeled.

Leech: the after edge of a sail.

Leeway: sideways motion through the water owing to the wind's pressure being on one side.

Limber hole: a hole in a frame or floor to allow bilge water to flow fore and aft.

Long and a short board: alternatively long and short tacks made to reach an objective not dead to windward.

Lubber's line: a mark inside a compass bowl to show the course being steered.

Luff: the forward edge of a sail; to turn the boat more nearly head to wind.

Lugsail: a quadrilateral sail supported by a spar not secured to the mast. *Balance lug:* one where the boom lies alongside the

147

mast like the yard. *Dipping lug:* one on which the sail and
yard have to be passed across every time the boat goes about.
Standing lug: a lug where the yard stays on one side of the mast
and the boom is on a goose-neck.

Main: the largest or principal sail; its mast or anything connected
with it.

Marline: thick twine used for serving. Often used tarred.

Miss stays: to fail in an attempt to go about.

Mitre: a diagonal band across the middle of a sail.

Mizzen: the aftermost mast, and its sail, where there is more
than one, and where it is not the main.

Mooring: a place where a boat is secured; tackle by which she is
anchored which is not weighed every time she leaves the berth.

Neap tide: tide whose range is at a minimum.

Oar: a device for propelling a boat by hand, using a rowlock or
other device as a fulcrum.

Outboard: outside the boat. *Outboard motor:* a portable motor,
with its own propeller, which can be fitted to the boat.

Overfalls: turbulent water due to the tidal stream running over
uneven bottom.

Paddle: a device, wholly supported in the hands, for propelling
a boat by hand.

Palm: the flat part on the fluke of an anchor; a pad worn on the
hand to press home a sail needle.

Parcelling: a spiral binding of tape or canvas round rope.

Pay off: to turn away from the wind.

Peak: the upper end of a gaff, or of the head of a gaff sail.

Pinching: sailing too close to the wind.

Pintle: the pin of a rudder's hangings which engages with the
gudgeon.

Pitch: to oscillate about a thwartships axis, bows alternately up
and down.

Planking: the wooden outer covering of the hull.

Popple: a small system of waves in confined waters.

Port: the left-hand side of a boat, looking from aft forward; an opening in the hull.

Preventer: a temporary or removable piece of rigging, usually a backstay.

Purchase: a system of blocks and line to give an increased pull; the amount of advantage so gained.

Quarter: the part of the hull on either side of the stern; the direction between astern and abeam.

Reach: to sail with the wind abeam.

Reef: to reduce the area of sail by rolling or tying down part of the sail. *Reef point:* a thin line with ends on each side of a sail to secure a reef.

Rib: the thwartships structural member of a hull. Usually used to mean bent timbers.

Rigging screws: screwed fittings for adjusting the tension in standing rigging.

Roach: the convex curvature of the leech or other edge of a sail.

Roll: to swing from side to side about a fore-and-aft axis.

Rove: threaded (through a block for instance); a washer over which a boat nail is clenched.

Rowlock: a crutch-shaped device serving as a fulcrum for an oar. In the Royal Navy called a crutch, rowlock being reserved for a notch in the sheerstrake serving the purpose.

Rubbing band: a strip round the outside of a hull to protect the planking.

Run: to sail with the wind aft.

Runner: a backstay which can be slid or released forward to make way for the boom.

Running rigging: rigging which renders through blocks or over sheaves to adjust and hoist sails and gear.

Scull: to propel a boat with one oar worked from side to side, using a notch or rowlock at the stern as a fulcrum.

Seam: a joint between two strakes.

Serving: a close-spaced binding, usually of marline, to protect rope from wear and weathering.

Shackle: a device consisting of a metal half-ring and a screwed pin, for joining rigging, fittings and chain.

Shank: the main straight part of an anchor.

Sheave: a wheel or pulley in a block or spar to make running gear.

Sheer: the line of the gunwale or deck edge.

Sheet: a line controlling the trim of a sail.

Shelf: a gunwale or inwale, usually used where deck beams are supported.

Ship: to fit in position on the boat.

Shroud: standing rigging giving lateral support to the mast.

Sit out: to move your weight outboard so as to keep the boat upright.

Spar: a pole supporting a sail or other gear.

Spinnaker: a very full sail used opposite the main when running.

Splice: to join rope by tucking the strands into one another.

Spreaders: struts holding shrouds out from the mast.

Spring tide: tide at the time of maximum range.

Stability: the quality by which a boat resists heeling forces.

Standing rigging: rigging supporting the masts, etc., which is permanently in position.

Starboard: the right-hand side looking from aft forward.

Stay: standing rigging giving fore-and-aft support; to go about.

Staysail: a sail which is hanked to a stay.

Stem: the foremost part of the boat; the outer structural member there. *Stem knee:* a knee inside the stem connecting apron and keelson.

Sternpost: the vertical backbone member right aft.

Stock: the cross-bar at the end of the shank of an anchor, remote from the crown; the upper part of the rudder, above the blade.

Strake: one plank of the hull. *Sheerstrake:* the uppermost strake. *Garboard strake:* the strake nearest the keel.

Stream: horizontal movement of the water.

Stringer: a fore-and-aft structural member.

Sweep: a long oar used on large boats.

Tack: a stretch of close-hauled sailing; to go about; to make progress to windward by making tacks; the forward lower corner of a sail. *Port tack:* close-hauled with the wind blowing from port to starboard. *Starboard tack:* close-hauled with the wind blowing from starboard to port.

Thimble: a metal ring or heart-shaped liner for a strop or eye-splice to protect it from chafe.

Throat: the lower end of a gaff; the upper forward corner of a gaff sail.

Thwart: a board across a boat, serving as a beam and as a seat.

Tide: vertical movement of the water caused by gravitational attraction by the sun and moon. *Tidal stream:* horizontal movement as a result of the tide.

Tide race: a region where tidal streams run very strongly, resulting in disturbed seas.

Tiller: the lever by which the rudder is controlled. *Tiller extension:* a hinged bar enabling the helmsman to steer while sitting out.

Timber: a frame or rib.

Tingle: a patch on the hull.

Topping lift: a line supporting the end of a boom.

Topsides: the sides of the hull between sheer and waterline.

Transit: two objects observed to be in line.

Transom: a flat end to the hull.

Trapeze: a belt slung from the mast to aid sitting out.

Traveller: a fitting consisting of a ring with a hook and shackle, which slides along a spar and has a sail or other spar hooked to it.

Trim: the fore-and-aft adjustment of the hull so that bow and stern are each immersed by the correct amount. To adjust the sheets.

Wake: the disturbed water which a boat leaves astern.

Warp: a stout line used for mooring or other purposes.

Wash: the waves set up by a boat's motion through the water.

GLOSSARY

Way: momentum of the boat. *Under way:* not moored, anchored, aground, or otherwise attached to the ground. *Having way on:* having momentum – i.e. moving through the water.

Weather: the windward side or direction. Opposite to lee.

Weigh: to raise an anchor off the bottom.

Whipping: a short binding on the end of a rope to prevent it from fraying.

Winch: a device having a drum operated by cranks or levers to give a mechanical advantage.

Windage: resistance due to the wind forces on hull, spars, rigging, etc.

Windward: towards the direction from which the wind is coming.

Worming: filling the grooves between strands of a rope with cord before parcelling.

Yacht: a vessel, not necessarily sailing, used for pleasure purposes.

Yard: a spar, other than a gaff, extending the head of a sail.